The New Corporatism: Social-Political Structures in the Iberian World. Fredrick B. Pike and Thomas Stritch, eds.

America in Change: Reflections on the 60's and 70's. Ronald Weber, ed.

Social Change in the Soviet Union. Boris Meissner, ed.

Foreign Assistance: A View from the Private Sector. Kenneth W. Thompson.

Hispanismo, 1898-1936: Spanish Conservatives and Liberals and Their Relations with Spanish America. Fredrick B. Pike.

Democracy in Crisis: New Challenges to Constitutional Democracy in the Atlantic Area. E. A. Goerner, ed.

The Task of Universities in a Changing World. Stephen D. Kertesz, ed.

The Church and Social Change in Latin America. Henry A. Landsberger, ed.

Revolution and Church: The Early History of Christian Democracy, 1789-1901. Hans Maier.

The Overall Development of Chile. Mario Zañartu, S.J., and John J. Kennedy, eds.

The Catholic Church Today: Western Europe. M. A. Fitzsimons, ed.

Contemporary Catholicism in the United States. Philip Gleason, ed.

The Major Works of Peter Chaadaev. Raymond T. McNally.

A Russian European: Paul Miliukov in Russian Politics. Thomas Riha.

A Search for Stability: U. S. Diplomacy Toward Nicaragua, 1925-1933. William Kamman.

Freedom and Authority in the West. George N. Shuster, ed.

Theory and Practice: History of a Concept from Aristotle to Marx. Nicholas Lobkowicz.

Coexistence: Communism and Its Practice in Bologna, 1945-1965. Robert H. Evans.

Marx and the Western World. Nicholas Lobkowicz, ed.

INTERNATIONAL STUDIES OF THE

COMMITTEE ON INTERNATIONAL RELATIONS

UNIVERSITY OF NOTRE DAME

Argentina's Foreign Policy 1930-1962. Alberto A. Conil Paz and Gustavo E. Ferrari.

Italy after Fascism, A Political History, 1943-1965. Guiseppe Mammarella.

The Volunteer Army and Allied Intervention in South Russia, 1917-1921. George A. Brinkley.

Peru and the United States, 1900-1962. James C. Carey.

Empire by Treaty: Britain and the Middle East in the Twentieth Century. M. A. Fitzsimons.

The USSR and the UN's Economic and Social Activities. Harold Karan Jacobson.

Death in the Forest: The Story of the Katyn Forest Massacre. J. K. Zawodny.

Chile and the United States: 1880-1962. Fredrick B. Pike.

Bolshevism: An Introduction to Soviet Communism, 2nd ed. Waldemar Gurian.

East Central Europe and the World: Developments in the Post-Stalin Era. Stephen D. Kertesz, ed.

Soviet Policy Toward International Control of Atomic Energy. Joseph L. Nogee.

The Russian Revolution and Religion, 1917-1925. Edited and translated by Boleslaw Szcześniak.

Introduction to Modern Politics. Ferdinand Hermens.

Freedom and Reform in Latin America. Fredrick B. Pike, ed.

What America Stands For. Stephen D. Kertesz and M. A. Fitzsimons, eds.

Theoretical Aspects of International Relations. William T. R. Fox, ed.

Catholicism, Nationalism and Democracy in Argentina. John J. Kennedy.

Why Democracies Fail. Norman L. Stamps.

German Protestants Face the Social Question. William O. Shanahan.

The Catholic Church in World Affairs. Waldemar Gurian and M. A. Fitzsimons, eds.

Diplomacy and Revolution

The Soviet Mission to Switzerland, 1918

by ALFRED ERICH SENN

UNIVERSITY OF NOTRE DAME PRESS

Notre Dame   London

Library of Congress Cataloging in Publication Data

Senn, Alfred Erich.
    Diplomacy and revolution.

    (International studies of the Committee on Inter-
national Relations, University of Notre Dame)
    Includes bibliographical references.
    1. Russia—Foreign relations—Switzerland.
2. Switzerland—Foreign relations—Russia. 3. Propaganda, Communist—Switzerland. I. Title. II. Series:
Notre Dame, Ind. University. Committee on International Relations. International studies.
DK67.5.S9S45   327.47'0494   73-22581
ISBN 0-268-00541-9

Manufactured in the United States of America

CONTENTS

Acknowledgments   ix

Introduction   1

1: BOLSHEVIK FOREIGN POLICY   5

2: SWISS NEUTRALITY   23

3: THE FIRST EMISSARIES   41

4: THE STRUGGLE FOR RECOGNITION   59

5: DIPLOMACY AND PARADIPLOMACY   79

6: PERSONALITIES AND ASSIGNMENTS   95

7: INFORMATION AND PROPAGANDA   111

8: THE GUILBEAUX AFFAIR   129

9: THE SPECTRE OF REVOLUTION   147

10: EXPULSION   161

Epilogue   179

Abbreviations   186

Notes   187

Note on Sources   211

Index   215

ACKNOWLEDGMENTS

Every book has its own history, and it is my pleasant duty here to offer my thanks to those who helped this one into existence. In particular I would like to mention Dr. Miroslav Tucek, Dr. Leonhard Haas, the late M. Jules Humbert-Droz, Prof. Georges Haupt, and Prof. George Brinkley. I also want to thank the staffs of the Swiss Bundesarchiv; the Schweizerisches Sozialarchiv, Zurich; the Zurich Staatsarchiv; the Landesbibliothek, Bern; the Staatsarchiv, Vienna; the Public Records Office, London; the Politisches Archiv des Auswärtigen Amtes, Bonn; and the Archives Historiques du Ministère de la Guerre, Vincennes, France. I completed much of the research under a grant from the Russian Area Studies Program of the University of Wisconsin.

I have received help and advice from many sources, but the ultimate responsibility for this work is of course mine alone.

INTRODUCTION

The Bolshevik Revolution of October 1917 in Russia constituted one of the major results of the First World War. Torn by the strains of the conflict, the Tsarist regime collapsed in February 1917, and in the resultant turmoil the Bolshevik party, led by Vladimir Ilich Lenin, emerged triumphant, bearing the standard of revolution. In challenging the world's economic structure, the Bolsheviks also collided with the diplomatic system set up by the Congress of Vienna. After first repudiating the Old Diplomacy, however, the Bolsheviks quickly adapted the manners and modes of diplomacy to their own revolutionary purposes.

In 1917 and 1918 the Bolshevik government established four major diplomatic missions abroad—in Berlin, Stockholm, London, and Bern. In many ways, the operation in Bern, headed by Jan Berzin, a veteran Latvian revolutionary, seemed the least important of these; most general surveys of the early years of Bolshevik foreign policy fail even to mention it. Nevertheless, the mission occupied an important place in the Bolsheviks' evaluation of the world revolutionary situation. In wartime Europe Switzerland held a unique place as a center of diplomatic intrigue; it had also sheltered the growing socialist movement against the war. In the absence of other channels for reaching France and Italy, Switzerland provided a useful base for the collection of information and the dissemination of revolutionary literature. The mission in Bern, furthermore, was the only Bolshevik diplomatic mission which by its own efforts won de facto recognition of the Soviet government from its host.

1

This study has attempted to examine the formation and operation of that mission. This has involved consideration of the development of Bolshevik thoughts on the character and methods of revolutionary diplomacy, the role of Switzerland as a center of both diplomatic and revolutionary activity, and also the Bolsheviks' problems in recruiting supporters and staffing their official institutions. A surprising conclusion of the study is the relatively minor significance of the mission for the question of direct Swiss-Soviet relations; in contrast to the situation at least in London and Berlin, relations with the host government, apart from the important question of recognition, seemed to be a matter of relatively low priority for the mission in Bern.

More important were its propaganda and informational goals. The mission, like the one previously established in Stockholm, had the prime purpose of publicizing and spreading the ideas and achievements of Bolshevik rule in Russia. Switzerland was not a major factor in international affairs; but Bolshevik leaders, experienced through years of exile in Western Europe, placed a high value on the ideological struggle in Switzerland which obviously would have repercussions in the neighboring states.

Examination of the mission's activities also illustrates the appeal which the Bolshevik revolution held for persons in Western Europe. For one reason or another, persons who scarcely even understood the term "Bolshevik" rallied to the support of the new government. In turn, the Bolsheviks sought to inform and to revolutionize these people.

Concerning the founding of the Comintern, Julius Braunthal has written that "of the forty-four delegates at the congress only five (Germany, Austria, Sweden, Norway and Holland) actually came in from abroad."[1] In fact, however, at least six of the delegates had worked with the mission in Switzerland. To this one can add the names of others such as Jules Humbert-Droz, Willi Münzenberg, and Jakob Herzog, prominent in the Comintern by 1920. The mission also recruited at least two persons who were later prominent in the Soviet diplomatic service.

The Soviet diplomatic mission in Bern worked closely with the International Socialist Commission in Stockholm. Organized in Switzerland during the war, the I.S.C. had moved to Stockholm in 1917 in order to be closer to the events in Russia, but after the Bolshevik revolution the I.S.C., now under Bolshevik leadership, turned its eyes back toward the West. In the fall of 1918 the secretary of the I.S.C. came to Switzerland, as a member of the Soviet mission, with the aim of establishing better contacts with the antiwar socialists in the Entente countries.

In this regard, the Soviet mission represented an important link between the antiwar Zimmerwald movement of 1914-1917 and the founding of the Comintern in 1919. Some western historians, to be sure, dispute or at least ignore the relationship between Zimmerwald and the Comintern, but Soviet historians draw the connection clearly. Five participants in the founding congress of the Comintern, including Lenin and Leon Trotsky, moreover, took the formal step of proclaiming the end of the Zimmerwald movement. One of them, Fritz Platten, had been intimately connected with the work of the Soviet mission in Bern.[2]

This is, to the best of my knowledge, the first effort in the West to study one of the four major Soviet diplomatic missions of 1918 using relevant diplomatic archives. Litvinov's mission in London has drawn the attention of a number of historians, but none of them have used the now available records in the Public Records Office.[3] The broad lines of Joffe's activity in Berlin have been described, but there are no studies specifically examining the policies and personnel of the mission in detail.[4] Vorovsky's mission in Stockholm has been often mentioned but never analyzed. The holdings of the Swiss Bundesarchiv, which form the basis of this study, are made up of both Swiss documents and also materials seized from the Russians in the fall of 1918. Several Swiss historians have already cited these materials, but their accounts have considered the mission mainly in the light of the Swiss General Strike of November 1918. They have made no attempt to examine the mission as a part of the development of Bolshevik foreign policy.[5]

In the last several years, Soviet historians have given great attention to early Soviet diplomatic history, and they have also used archival sources in considering the activity of the various missions abroad. In the case of the mission in Bern, the results so far have indicated that the documentation available in Switzerland is superior to that which the Soviet historians have at their command.[6] The Soviet studies also differ generally from western analyses by their insistence on distinguishing the diplomatic and the revolutionary policies of the Bolshevik regime.[7] In my opinion this distinction cannot be so clearly drawn; in 1918 the Soviet government's diplomatic moves and its hopes for world revolution represented an integral whole and must be studied as such.

1: BOLSHEVIK FOREIGN POLICY

On June 21, 1918, a Soviet diplomatic mission opened for business in Bern, the capital of Switzerland. By its success in taking over the residence of the former Imperial Russian legation, it had won de facto recognition from the Swiss government, and it had established the Soviet government's claim to be the successor of the fallen Tsarist regime. At the same time, as the fourth link in the small chain of Soviet diplomatic representations—missions had previously been organized in Stockholm, London, and Berlin—the mission in Bern held no illusions about its place in the diplomatic world. While claiming traditional diplomatic privileges and immunities, the Soviet representatives viewed themselves more as being accredited to the workers of Switzerland and western Europe than to the Swiss government. The Soviet regime in Russia considered itself the harbinger of a new social order which would soon be realized through world revolution.

The establishment and the operation of the Soviet mission in Bern offered a striking example of diplomatic and revolutionary improvisation. The government's instructions to the minister, Jan Berzin, were very general; moreover, Berzin was at first subordinated in some degree to the major diplomatic mission in Berlin, headed by Adolf A. Joffe. Nevertheless Berzin and his staff displayed considerable initiative in adapting their work both to the developing situation in Russia and to the specific conditions of Switzerland. Indeed, some persons nominally under Berzin's direction, such as Ivan Zalkind, displayed so much initiative that they seemed virtually independent even of their chief. Behind the

5

mission's work lay eight months of experience on the part of a revolutionary regime; the Bolsheviks had learned painfully, by trial and error, the differences between revolutionary theory and the realities of power.

Western diplomats in Switzerland could not comprehend the scope and the character of Bolshevik activities. They could not perceive the genuine appeal which the Bolshevik revolution held for western radicals and liberals, and they believed that the Soviet leaders had allied themselves with the Germans. International social revolution, while a threatening prospect, seemed a chimera of German-Bolshevik intrigues. Their judgment clouded by the passions of war, the diplomats failed to understand even the basic principles of Soviet foreign policy.

When the Bolsheviks came to power in Russia in November 1917, they proclaimed their rejection of the old social order not only in Russia but throughout the world. The Tsarist regime had collapsed in February 1917 as the result of the strains of thirty months of war, but its successor, the Provisional Government, had proved incapable, under either liberal or socialist leadership, of resolving those strains. Vladimir Ilich Lenin, the leader of the Bolshevik party, had predicted this failure, declaring that the socialist revolution must not just seize the apparatus of bourgeois government; it must destroy that apparatus and build anew. Bolshevik rule, therefore, both brought new concepts to the conduct of foreign relations and also meant a complete reorganization of the institutions of Russian foreign policy.

On November 8, 1917, as one of its first official acts, the Bolshevik government issued its Decree on Peace, calling upon the belligerent powers "immediately to begin negotiations for a just and democratic peace," without annexations and without indemnities. The decree defined annexations as being "any incorporation into a large or powerful state of a small or weak nationality without the definitely, clearly, and voluntarily expressed consent and will of this population, regardless of when this forcible incorporation was accomplished." The slogan thereby meant far more than simply a return to the boundaries of 1914. The Bolsheviks were calling upon the Great Powers to renounce their colonies and even to revise their old frontiers as part of the peace settlement, although the decree added that this was not meant to be "an ultimatum." In addition, the decree anticipated that "all peoples and nationalities, without exception," would take part in the peace negotiations and that "plenipotentiary assemblies of people's representatives of all countries" would eventually ratify the settlement.

The Bolsheviks directed the decree to both the "belligerent peoples" and "their governments." Appealing more directly to the "class conscious workers of the three most advanced nations of the world," i.e., England, France, and Germany, the document expressed confidence that the workers "will understand the tasks devolving upon them of saving mankind from the horrors of war and its consequences."[1]

In his explanatory comments on the decree, Lenin repeated that the Bolsheviks did not want their conditions of peace to be considered an ultimatum. The government stood ready to consider all counterproposals: "We will examine them, but this does not mean that we will accept them." At the same time, Lenin made clear that he was concerned about the attitude of the long-suffering Russian peasant. The peasant must be shown that the capitalist governments cannot make peace; Lenin promised to bring any counteroffers from other states to the consideration of the Constituent Assembly, then being elected in Russia. Lenin also emphasized that the decree represented a new style of diplomacy. The Bolsheviks had addressed their appeal to both governments and peoples: "Everywhere governments and peoples are at odds, and therefore we must help the peoples to intervene in questions of war and peace."[2]

The Decree on Peace also announced the abolition of secret diplomacy and the intention of the new government to publish the secret treaties concluded by the Provisional Government with its allies. Lenin declared that the government would send the decree "everywhere," so that all people would know of it and of the workers' and peasants' revolution in Russia. The Bolsheviks would not allow the capitalist governments to conceal the news of the revolution and of its accomplishments.

On November 22 the Bolsheviks completed the first stage of their diplomatic revolution by proceeding to publish secret documents from the archives of the Tsarist and Provisional Governments. Secret diplomacy, Leon Trotsky declared, had served the interests of only the minority ruling classes, and its abolition represented "the very first condition of honesty for national, truly democratic foreign policy." Therefore the Workers' and Peasants' Government "abolished secret diplomacy with its intrigues, ciphers, and falsehood." The Bolsheviks sought the "quickest possible peace on the basis of honest coexistence and cooperation of nations. We want the quickest possible overthrow of the rule of capital."[3]

Behind the Decree on Peace lay years of revolutionary polemics as well as a relatively recent compromise in the views of Lenin and Leon Trotsky, two veteran antagonists in the Russian revolutionary movement. In 1914 Trotsky had advocated "immediate peace without annexations and without indemnities," but Lenin had argued that the war was a natural expression of the conflicts within the capitalist system; therefore no lasting peace was possible so long as capitalism continued to exist and pacifistic calls for an end to hostilities only served to delude the workers. The true socialist should call for the conversion of the imperialist war into a civil war, a revolutionary war. Trotsky argued to the contrary that the call for peace was itself a revolutionary action, and he insisted that his slogan was correct. In 1915 and 1916, recognizing the emotional appeal of the call for peace, Lenin came to accept the slogan, but he interpreted it in his own way.

Writing in the fall of 1915 Lenin declared that the first action of the "party of the proletariat" upon taking power should be to "propose peace to all the belligerents on the basis of the liberation of the colonies and of all the dependent, oppressed, and disenfranchised peoples." Given the nature of capitalism neither of the warring camps could accept such a demand, and the revolutionary government would then "have to prepare for and wage a revolutionary war; i.e., we would not only, by resolute measures, fully carry out the whole of our minimum program, but we would also systematically rouse all the peoples now oppressed by the Great Russians, all the colonies and dependent countries in Asia (India, China, Persia, etc.), to insurrection, and primarily we would rouse the socialist proletariat of Europe to insurrection against the governments and in spite of its social chauvinists." In March 1916 he amplified his understanding of "annexation" by insisting that a socialist must "demand the immediate and unconditional *freedom of separation* for all colonies and nations oppressed by his own 'fatherland.' "[4]

On these terms, Lenin and Trotsky could agree on a peace program in 1917. For neither of them, however, did the program represent a will for a separate peace with Germany. Lenin had repeatedly declared his opposition to a separate peace. In a speech given in July, he stated, "When they say that we seek a separate peace, that is untrue. We say, 'No separate peace with any capitalists, least of all with Russians.' The Provisional Government has made a separate peace with Russian capitalists. Down with this separate peace! We recognize no separate peace with the German capitalists, and we will enter into no talks, but also no separate peace with the English and French imperialists."

In a newspaper article of September, however, Lenin took a more cautious view of a separate peace, declaring that his proposed call for a general peace would "not be met by the good will of the capitalists." The excitement of the people would nevertheless force the capitalists to act, and if the "least probable" possibility should occur and "not one" warring power would accept the proposal of an armistice, then revolutionary war would be necessary. Under such circumstances, the Russian war effort would be "many times stronger," since it would represent a war "in union with the oppressed classes of all countries."[5]

The Bolsheviks entered upon their revolution with the image of a worldwide socialist revolution which would destroy the capitalist governments and would tear down old frontiers. They specifically rejected old concepts of international relations, and Trotsky, as the new People's Commissar of Foreign Affairs, lost no opportunity to make this clear. "I will issue a few revolutionary proclamations to the peoples of the world," he reportedly declared, "and then shut up shop." Traditional diplomacy had no more place in this view of the world than did the idea of a separate peace.[6]

On November 21, thirteen days after the proclamation of the Decree on Peace, Trotsky delivered notes to the diplomatic representatives of Russia's erstwhile allies—England, France, and the United States—calling on them to regard the decree as a proposal for an "immediate armistice on all fronts and the immediate opening of peace talks." The western diplomats, however, were disinclined to recognize the Bolshevik government, and they gave no response.

In fulfillment of their program the Bolsheviks also issued a Declaration of the Rights of the Peoples of Russia. Proclaiming a policy of "voluntary and honest union of the peoples of Russia," the declaration affirmed the "right of the peoples of Russia to free self-determination, even to the point of separation and the formation of an independent state." The Bolsheviks hereby agreed in principle to the disintegration of the Russian state. On December 3 the Council of People's Commissars added an appeal to the Moslems of Russia, Persia, Turkey, India, and the Arab lands to rise against the imperialists.[7]

The Bolshevik Revolution also shattered the structure of the old Ministry of Foreign Affairs. The Provisional Government had changed relatively few faces in the ministry, and the personnel openly opposed the Bolshevik coup. On November 29 the Bolsheviks dismissed all recalcitrant workers, and on December 5, the government ordered all Russia's diplomatic representatives abroad to declare whether or not they supported the new regime. Only two eventually came into the service of the Soviet government.

As Trotsky became involved in general governmental affairs, the routine conduct of the work of the Commissariat of Foreign Affairs fell to his deputy, Ivan Abramovich Zalkind, an old Bolshevik who held a doctorate in biology from the Sorbonne. During the war he had lived in Algeria and in Spain; after returning to Russia in 1917, he had played an important role in the Bolshevik success in his native Petrograd. In addition to assuming such tasks as breaking up the strike of the former employees of the Foreign Ministry, Zalkind also served as editor of *Die Fackel,* a newspaper published for German and other foreign prisoners of war in Russia. When Lenin received western diplomats on January 14, Zalkind represented the Commissariat. The diplomats generally disliked him; a French diplomat called him "nervous, impulsive, and sometimes brutish." A friend, however, characterized him as "a handsome man," who, "with his long delicate face, slender build and sensitive hands," had an "aristocratic" appearance: "Nevertheless he was one of the sincerest revolutionists that I knew."[8]

The relations between the Bolsheviks and the western diplomats, strained from the beginning, became increasingly delicate as the Bolsheviks appealed directly to the German government to open talks on an armistice. The Germans had long desired a settlement on their Eastern Front, and on November 27 Berlin agreed.

The Bolsheviks found themselves forced step by step toward a separate peace with Germany. They turned to the western diplomats in Petrograd with an appeal for the Allies to join in the talks; they sent radio broadcasts to governments and peoples, but to no avail. Lenin repeatedly expressed faith in the growing revolutionary feeling of the masses in the warring states, but the masses in turn failed to demonstrate this growth. When the Soviet government agreed to separate talks with the Germans, it still hoped that something else would develop. As Trotsky put it, "If the peoples of Europe do not arise and crush imperialism, we shall be crushed—that is beyond doubt."[9]

On December 2 the Bolshevik and German delegations sat down together at Brest-Litovsk behind the German lines, and on the fifteenth they reached agreement on an armistice.[10] The Soviet government still appealed to "the toiling masses of all countries" to come to the help of the socialist revolution, but on December 22 it began formal peace negotiations with the Central Powers, again at Brest-Litovsk.

The Bolsheviks carried their revolutionary conceptions of international relations to the bargaining table, but they found the representatives of the Central Powers unyielding. The head of the Bolshevik delegation, A. A. Joffe, proposed agreement on the conditions of no annexations, no indemnities, and recognition of the right of national self-determination, and on Christmas Day the Germans seemingly accepted. The Bolsheviks rejoiced, but the Germans then declared that the peoples of the territories occupied by the Central Powers had already declared their desire to be independent of Russia. The Russians were thunderstruck; one Bolshevik reportedly even wept. Bolshevik oratory failed in this first effort to overwhelm the German military, and the talks adjourned on December 28.

The Soviet government now renewed its own appeal to both governments and workers in the Entente countries. The Bolshevik proposals, it announced, embodied "consistent socialist democracy," which could unite all nations in "economic and cultural cooperation." Should the Entente governments continue to boycott the peace talks, "the working class will be faced by the iron necessity of seizing power from the hands of those who cannot or will not give peace to peoples!" In one and the same document, the Soviet government appealed to the Entente governments to join in the peace talks and to the working classes to turn on the capitalists "under the banner of peace, the brotherhood of nations and socialist reconstruction of society."[11]

In their attempts to reach the working masses of the Entente countries, the Bolsheviks faced enormous difficulties. The hostile attitude of the foreign diplomats in Petrograd meant that all official channels of communication were closed, and beyond the use of radio waves, the Bolsheviks had to rely on their agents and friends in Stockholm to transmit their message.

Even before coming to power, the Bolsheviks had

maintained a foreign bureau in Stockholm. During the war a significant antiwar movement had developed in Switzerland, and in 1917, after the February revolution in Russia, the central organ of this "Zimmerwald movement," the International Socialist Commission (I.S.C.), had moved to Stockholm in order to be closer to the exciting events in Petrograd. To be sure, the commission had at first been headed by the Swiss socialist Robert Grimm, who had determinedly opposed Lenin, but in the summer of 1917, the commission passed into the hands of Angelica Balabanova, who delivered it into Lenin's camp: "Whatever my personal difference with the opinions of some of the Bolshevik leaders, it seemed to me at this time, as to a number of other Marxists, who had never been Bolsheviks, that the salvation of the Russian Revolution lay with the tendency which they represented."[12] As a result, in November 1917, the Bolsheviks turned naturally to Stockholm as their window to the West.

As its first representative abroad, the Soviet government chose Vatslav V. Vorovsky, a journalist then resident in Stockholm. Although he entered upon his duties in November, Vorovsky's formal notice of appointment was dated December 6. "The matter is not being an envoy to the Swedish king or government," he was instructed, "but being a diplomatic agent of Soviet power, located in Stockholm but empowered to establish ties and conduct talks not so much with Sweden as through Sweden with other countries...."[13] In the words of a leading Soviet official, Vorovsky, although unrecognized by the Swedish government, "tirelessly carried out his task of relations with the Swedish proletariat and with all foreign European groups of workers standing on the side of the Russian October Revolution."[14]

Vorovsky worked closely with Balabanova, and at

first he even shared the offices of the I.S.C. When Vorovsky was out of Stockholm, Balabanova "had to act as his substitute. . . . It was a time when Russia was attempting to buy agricultural and other necessary machinery in Sweden, and in the absence of Vorovsky the negotiations between the Swedish firms and the Russian agents who came to Stockholm for this purpose were left in my hands."[15]

The I.S.C. itself was at this point virtually an organ of the Bolshevik party and the Soviet government. As Balabanova put it, "to our propaganda for immediate peace, based upon concerted action of the working class, was now added the additional task of mobilizing the working-class opinion throughout the world to the defence of the Russian Revolution."[16]

On December 26 the Soviet press carried the announcement that the government had placed two million rubles at the disposition "of the representatives abroad of the Commissariat of Foreign Affairs for the needs of the revolutionary movement." This money was to aid "the left, internationalist wing of the workers' movement of all countries, whether these countries are at war with Russia or are allied with her or whether they are remaining neutral." The Commissariat then assigned the money to Vorovsky's mission in Stockholm for distribution.[17]

According to Balabanova, Soviet couriers carried virtually unlimited funds to Stockholm. "But I beg you," Lenin reportedly wrote, "don't economize. Spend millions, many many millions."[18] The major problem in the distribution of the funds apparently lay in the difficulty of transferring the money from Sweden to the other countries of war torn Europe.

As valuable as Vorovsky's and Balabanova's work was, the Soviet government still sought to expand its contacts with the working classes in the West. Immediately after the October Revolution, the Bolsheviks had established an international department under the All-Russian Central Executive Committee of the Congress of Soviets. The department's task was to enter into "relations with the foreign revolutionary movement." On December 20 the Council of People's Commissars decided to send a delegation abroad for this purpose, and on January 4, 1918, the Central Executive Committee declared that the delegation should take "preparatory steps for calling an international conference of representatives of the left wing of the International accepting Soviet power and the necessity of struggle for immediate peace against the imperialist governments within each warring country." The delegation should also inform the masses of Western Europe about the events within Soviet Russia. For the time being, however, the project went no further than the planning stage, and the government deferred naming the members of the delegation.[19]

At the end of December, as the news of the tough German stand at Brest-Litovsk reached Petrograd, the Bolsheviks chose to make a more direct approach to the western public by naming diplomatic representatives in England and in Switzerland. Maxim Litvinov, who had once represented the Bolshevik party in the International Socialist Bureau of the Second International, became Russia's Plenipotentiary Representative in London, and Viacheslav Karpinsky, who had long directed the Bolsheviks' publishing activities in Geneva, became the envoy to Switzerland. Both men were still living in the emigration, and the Soviet government arranged with the Entente representatives in Petrograd for a diplomatic courier, Eduard Holzmann, to carry instructions and credentials to them.[20]

Despite these moves the Entente powers remained unresponsive to the calls for general peace. On January

8, 1918, President Woodrow Wilson of the United States issued his list of fourteen points as a basis for peace, including a call for the withdrawal of all foreign troops from Russian soil; but the western capitals gave no direct answers to the Bolshevik appeals. The Allied silence and—more important in Lenin's view—the passivity of the working classes to the Bolsheviks' exhortations led the Soviet government further toward a separate peace.

The new phase of the peace talks with the Germans began on January 9, as Trotsky took charge of the Bolshevik delegation with the aim of playing for time by dragging out the negotiations. After ten days of rhetorical duels, the Germans cut short the debate by unfolding a map and delineating Germany's territorial demands; there was nothing more to discuss. The talks again adjourned to allow Trotsky to return to Petrograd for instructions.

Lenin now considered it impossible to proclaim a "revolutionary war." Russia needed a "breathing space," he argued; the Soviet government needed time to consolidate itself and the army needed time to reorganize. Heartened by news of popular disturbances in Vienna and Berlin, he recommended drawing out the negotiations as long as possible but he made clear his own view that it "would be absolutely impermissible to risk the fate of the socialist revolution which has already begun in Russia" on the chance that revolution would soon come to Germany. Faced by a German ultimatum, Russia would have to sign a separate peace.[21]

At this time the Bolshevik government gave new emphasis to its developing role as a state among states by reorganizing the Commissariat of Foreign Affairs and expanding its representation abroad. After long delays, two leading socialist emigrés, Georgii Chicherin and Peter Petrov, had finally succeeded in returning from

England. Chicherin, who only now joined the Bolshevik party, assumed the post of Deputy Commissar of Foreign Affairs, and he gradually took over the direction of the Commissariat from Trotsky and Zalkind. Petrov took the post of chairman of the international department of the Central Executive Committee and worked closely with Chicherin.

At the end of January the government named L. B. Kamenev, formerly a member of the delegation at Brest-Litovsk, as its representative in Paris, and ordered Zalkind to Switzerland as a replacement for Karpinsky, who had now returned to Russia. Through chance, Raymond Robins, an American Red Cross official who advocated a friendly American attitude toward the Bolsheviks, chose this moment to complain to Lenin about some discourtesy on Zalkind's part. Lenin, seeing an opportunity to impress Robins with his amiability, questioned whether he would object to Zalkind's being sent to Bern. Relishing his apparent victory, Robins joked, "Thank you, Mr. Lenin. As I can't send the son of a bitch to hell, 'burn' is the next best thing you can do with him."[22] Robins undoubtedly overestimated the effectiveness of his protest.

As Trotsky then returned to Brest-Litovsk at the end of January, his government was going through a process of change perhaps greater than even he realized. Trotsky probably clung longer to the visions of November than did Lenin and the new generation of administrators in the Commissariat of Foreign Affairs. Trotsky later insisted that he had been acting in agreement with Lenin and that he had supported the Bolshevik leader against those who wanted to proclaim a revolutionary war. But Lenin accepted Trotsky's intention of dragging out the negotiations only to the point of a possible German ultimatum; at that point Lenin stood ready to sign a peace.

At Brest-Litovsk the Germans would tolerate no more delay, and on February 10, attempting to preempt an ultimatum, Trotsky announced Russia's demobilization. The conditions posed by the Central Powers, he declared, were unacceptable: "We are going out of the war, but we feel ourselves compelled to refuse to sign the peace treaty." The Germans were nonplused, and Trotsky left for home in the belief that his bold stroke had triumphed. In Petrograd the Central Executive Committee endorsed his action, but on February 16 the news came that the Germans were resuming hostilities.

The Russian army could offer no resistance, and the Germans advanced 150 miles in six days. Even Petrograd seemed endangered; the Bolsheviks hastily arranged the removal of the government to Moscow, where it was in fact to remain.

The combination of developments—the demoralization of the Russian army and the willingness of the Germany army to march against the revolution—brought a profound crisis to the Bolsheviks. Trotsky's actions now came into a different light, and Soviet historians have criticized him for having opened Russia to the German invasion. Trotsky turned to the Allies for help, but while the diplomats replied in encouraging fashion, their governments proved less than enthusiastic. Russia stood alone, and faced by demands for a revolutionary war, Lenin needed all his enormous persuasive talents to win his party's agreement to signing a peace treaty with the Germans, a peace now even more onerous than that which Trotsky had rejected.

The signing of the peace at Brest-Litovsk on March 3 completed the process whereby the Soviet government evolved from its first revolutionary pronouncements of November 1917 to its acceptance of the principle of diplomatic relations with the capitalist states. Lenin painstakingly explained that signing the peace was analogous to losing a strike, that it did not mean a "deal" with the Germans. The government named Joffe as its plenipotentiary representative to Berlin, and since Joffe had opposed signing the peace, his nomination embodied the view that Soviet Russia was only seeking a "breathing space." Nevertheless, Soviet Russia had now agreed to receive a representative of the Imperial German government; the revolutionary war had been delayed.

In his original program of 1915 for a revolutionary foreign policy, Lenin had written of the necessity "to prepare for and wage a revolutionary war." On the other hand, he had specified a second vital part of his program; namely, that of arousing "the socialist proletariat of Europe to insurrection against its government." The Treaty of Brest-Litovsk, he now argued, meant no change in the basic aims of the Bolshevik party; everything would just take more time. Waging a revolutionary war was out of the question: "To embark on the adventure of an armed rising, when it is knowingly an adventure, is unworthy of a Marxist."[23] It remained for the Bolsheviks to prepare for the next phase of the revolution.[24]

On February 6 the Soviet government had taken a step toward "preparing for a revolutionary war" as the Commissariat of Foreign Affairs played host to a gathering of foreign socialists. The group issued a call for an international socialist conference of parties and organizations advocating "revolutionary struggle against their own governments on behalf of immediate peace," and declaring "support of the October Russian Revolution and of the Soviet government." The group had originally intended to constitute itself as such a conference, but it had given up on this when Angelica Balabanova could not make the trip from Stockholm. In her absence, the

group decided to serve only as a preliminary conference.[25]

In mid-February the Bolsheviks finally named the
delegation planned some weeks earlier by the Central
Executive Committee. Including Jan Berzin, Mark
Natanson, and Alexandra Kollontaj, the delegation was
to establish an information bureau in Stockholm, working closely with the International Socialist Commission,
and also to publish an "informational organ" to be
entitled "Messenger of the Socialist Revolution." The
group was also to enter into contact "with all elements
of the workers' movement and with parties which are
carrying on an active revolutionary struggle for an immediate peace and which support the point of view of
the quickest possible social revolution."[26] Berzin was
now appointed a diplomatic courier to France, England,
Norway, Sweden, and the United States.

The delegation, however, found it impossible to
travel to Stockholm, and its plan of activity had to be
abandoned. In Balabanova's words, the I.S.C. remained
"the link between Russia and the socialists of the left in
various countries."[27] To this, of course, must be added
the new Soviet diplomatic service.

The Bolshevik revolution had failed to bring down
the European state system, and now Lenin forced his
party and his government to accommodate itself, however temporarily, to that system. As the Bolsheviks
adjusted to this prospect, they turned their eyes toward
Switzerland. Ironically, the Zimmerwald movement, as
personified by the I.S.C., had left that country in 1917
in an effort to be closer to the events and developments
in Russia. Now, under new direction, it began to consider the reverse process. As the official Soviet government newspaper *Izvestiia* commented, the slogans of the
proletarian revolution could find fertile soil in the neu-

tral countries as well as in the warring countries. Propaganda activity in these countries, moreover, could be conducted more easily than in the territory of the belligerents because the bourgeoisie had not yet succeeded in establishing a military dictatorship.[28]

Stockholm was too isolated for contact with the key Entente countries of Italy and France. In February 1918 both Balabanova and Vorovsky notified comrades in Switzerland of the coming of Bolshevik agents and representatives and of the anticipated expansion of Bolshevik activities there. Long a center for international movements, Switzerland was now about to play host for yet another one.

2: SWISS NEUTRALITY

Wartime Switzerland found neutrality a precious but evanescent commodity. When war came in 1914, the government proclaimed its neutrality and ordered the army mobilized to defend the frontier. Elected as the commander in chief of the army was Colonel Ulrich Wille, who had received his training in Germany and possessed a decoration from the Kaiser. (The Swiss army, it might be noted, had no generals in peace time; Wille was now raised to the rank of general.) In the next few months, rising passions in French West Switzerland and in German East Switzerland raised the spectre of a serious split, but by the end of the year Swiss patriotism had prevailed. An address entitled "Our Swiss Standpoint," delivered to the New Helvetic Society in Zurich by the poet Carl Spitteler early in December, seemed to mark the turning point. National tensions continued throughout the war, but the unity of the Swiss Confederation was not seriously threatened.

At several points, particularly in 1915 when Italy entered the war and again in 1916 when a case of German intrigue within the Swiss General Staff gave rise to anti-German demonstrations throughout Switzerland but especially in the West, the delicate balance between Switzerland's nationalities seemed threatened. In 1917 the "Grimm affair," which the British minister labeled "a breach of neutrality," posed a new threat to Switzerland's position between the belligerents.

In May 1917 Robert Grimm, as head of the I.S.C., had traveled to Russia and, on his own initiative, had undertaken to act as an intermediary between the Russian Provisional Government and the Germans. In a

telegram to the Swiss Foreign Minister, Arthur Hoffmann, Grimm reported, "There is a general desire for
peace." Hoffmann responded, "I have become convinced that Germany is seeking a peace with Russia,
honorable for both sides," and he went on to list some
of Germany's general aims in the East.

Unfortunately for Grimm, Entente agents came
into possession of the two telegrams, and they brought
to the Russian government the charge that Grimm was a
German agent. Grimm's friends, who knew nothing of
his efforts to act as a go-between, attempted at first to
defend him, but as the facts of the exchange became
clear, they were rendered impotent. The Russian government expelled Grimm from the country.

The net result of the crisis was a major victory for
the Bolsheviks and a minor victory for the Entente. In
the aftermath of Grimm's disgrace, Balabanova had
taken over the I.S.C. and had delivered it into the
Bolshevik camp. On the other hand, Hoffmann resigned
his post, and the Entente diplomats accepted the explanation that the Swiss government bore no responsibility
for the affair.[1]

The warring powers themselves encouraged internal
divisions in Switzerland, since the Swiss situation repre-
sented both opportunity and danger for all concerned.
A British diplomatic report noted, "It would be desir-
able to warn British subjects coming to Switzerland to
be careful not to patronize hotels in the hands of per-
sons of German origin who probably are mostly spies."
The Russians estimated that all the large hotels of
French Switzerland were in the hands of Germans. The
Germans complained that pro-French agents among the
Swiss police regularly warned Entente agents, and the
Austrians considered the French Swiss more pro-
Entente than the German-Swiss were pro-German. A
British observer, to the contrary, argued that "a Ger-
man-Swiss is a German first and a Swiss afterwards."[2]

The foreign diplomats all looked askance at the seven member Bundesrat, the federal executive organ of the Swiss government. The Entente diplomats viewed the four German members at the end of 1917 as suspect, and they particularly considered Eduard Müller, who headed the Police and Justice Department, and Edmund Schulthess, head of the Department of National Economy, as pro-German. The British envoy said of Schulthess, who had been president in 1917, "I consider that we have an enemy in Mr. Schulthess." A British intelligence report of October 1918 declared of Schulthess and former Bundesrat Arthur Hoffmann, "It is not too much to say that they were acting simply as Bolshevik agents."[3]

The Germans, on the other hand, disliked the two French Swiss and the one Italian Swiss in the council: Gustave Ador, head of the Interior Department, Camille Decoppet, head of the Military Department, and Giuseppe Motta, head of Finance and Customs. Ador, who was the head of the International Red Cross, had succeeded Hoffmann in the Bundesrat, and his clear preference for the cause of the Entente made his presence in the government particularly upsetting for the Germans.

The presidency, which changed hands annually, fell in 1918 to Dr. Felix Ludwig Calonder, a German Swiss, whom the British envoy, Sir Horace Rumbold, had earlier criticized as pro-German. When Calonder took office in January, however, Rumbold, in a rather typical wartime turnabout, considered him to be pro-Entente. The American minister, Pleasant A. Stovall, speculated, however, that Calonder would be inclined, under German pressure, to recognize the Bolshevik regime in Russia. In the course of the year, the Germans became increasingly critical of Calonder, complaining that they had no influence on him because he was "especially sensitive." A Bavarian agent in Switzerland angrily reported that Calonder "is showing himself to be weak and not inaccessible to certain influences of the Entente."[4]

The Swiss government expressed great pride in its tradition of neutrality. In 1914 the *Neue Zürcher Zeitung* proclaimed that unlike Belgian neutrality, which was an "artificial machination of the European powers," Swiss neutrality represented "a self-chosen policy corresponding to the specific conditions and the central location of the country and exercised for centuries."[5] The warring powers, however, tended to be blind to the virtue of neutrality. They recognized Swiss neutrality only after being assured that the Swiss would defend themselves against an invading army, and then they maintained their own watch over political and economic developments in the country.

For all their complaints about the Swiss, the foreign missions did not refrain from their own breaches of neutrality.[6] Switzerland indeed became a hotbed of intrigue and espionage as each warring power maintained its own intelligence network in the country, more often than not under the direction of the military attaché. Probably the most elaborate apparatuses belonged to the Germans and the French.

In February 1918 the French stiffened their posture in Bern as they named a new envoy, Paul Dutasta, who reputedly was the personal nominee of French Premier Georges Clemenceau and was charged with the task of putting greater pressure on the Swiss to follow a pro-Entente policy. With Dutasta came a new military attaché, Colonel Pageot, who had once before already held that post. Under Pageot's leadership, the Entente military attachés pooled their information, and Pageot's reports often served virtually as news releases, being frequently repeated in British and even Swiss intelligence reports. Despite Pageot's influence in certain

Swiss circles, however, in October 1918 he complained, "Up to now my relations with Swiss courts, advantageous in other respects, have been in a way unilateral. I have furnished them with many reports on this question [i.e., foreign revolutionaries in Switzerland]. They have never acted reciprocally."[7]

The German mission in Bern had been headed since 1912 by Gisbert von Romberg, who had won for himself a place in world history by agreeing to Lenin's request for permission to return to Russia through Germany in April 1917. Although some historians have claimed that he had long maintained a special relationship with the Russian Bolsheviks, the documents of his mission indicate that he had little to do with Russian socialists before the spring of 1917. The German military attaché, Major Herbert von Bismarck, a nephew of the Iron Chancellor, maintained a network of informants among the numerous Russian emigrés, but the major thrust of his work seemed to be directed at France.[8]

The Entente powers differed sharply in their evaluations of Romberg and Bismarck. The English considered Bismarck "a notorious organizer of espionage and 'defeatism' in France and Italy," and they thought Romberg "harmless."[9] While Pageot spoke darkly of depraved practices among the members of the German mission, another French agent called Romberg "extremely formidable" and declared that Bismarck "didn't amount to much."[10] In general, the other attachés demonstrated considerable respect for Bismarck's work although they of course rejoiced when he was compromised by being connected with the efforts of Italian anarchists to smuggle bombs and propaganda materials out of Switzerland.

The fortunes of war and revolution had wrought great changes in the Russian mission. Vasily Romanovich Bakherakht, who had served as Russia's envoy since 1906, was the doyen of the diplomatic corps in Bern at the time of his death in October 1916. Mikhail M. Bibikov, who had joined the mission in 1914 after leaving a post in Munich, served as chargé d'affaires until the February Revolution in Russia. Closely associated with the Tsarist intelligence service in Switzerland, Bibikov was the target of considerable protest on the part of the emigrés, and the Provisional Government discharged him in March. Rumors current in Switzerland in 1918 associated Bibikov, who had disobeyed orders to return to Russia after his dismissal, and Bakherakht's widow with German intrigues. Bibikov angrily denied these stories as "common slanders and gross insulting lies," but in fact he apparently received as much as 10,000 Swiss francs per month from the Austrians.[11]

After the February Revolution in Russia, the mission had fallen into the hands of Andrei Mikhailovich Onu, the First Secretary, who continued to serve on a temporary basis into the summer of 1918. He apparently owed his position to the support of the Entente diplomats in Bern. S. G. Svatikov, the head of a special commission appointed by the Provisional Government to investigate the work of the Tsarist secret police in Western Europe, filed a series of complaints against Onu, charging him with systematically impeding the work of the commission and also with tolerating the development of a counterrevolutionary movement which was seeking to restore the monarchy in Russia with the help of the Germans.[12]

Onu, on the other hand, drew the warm endorsement of the American minister, who called him "a man with whom I have always had most pleasant relations."[13] When the Bolsheviks announced the dismissal of the old diplomatic corps, Onu followed the lead of the heads of other Russian missions in Western Europe in looking to the Russian ambassador in Paris, V. A. Maklakov, as their center for coordinating actions and policies.[14]

Two other key Russian diplomatic posts in Switzerland showed no change as a result of the fall of the Tsarist government. The military attaché, General S. A. Golovan, had assumed his post in 1915 when his predecessor had become "careless." He remained at his post throughout 1917 despite some complaints among the emigré community. Stranger still was the case of Leon A. Gornostaev, Russian Consul General in Geneva since August 1916, who had directed surveillance of political emigrés in French Switzerland and had even operated a Russian spy network on the Riviera. Despite repeated complaints and petitions by the emigrés in Geneva, the Provisional Government failed to recall him.

In all, the Russian diplomatic institutions in Switzerland lacked the confidence of the majority of the several thousand Russian citizens living in the country; they could not claim to represent either the Provisional Government or the Bolshevik regime. Onu's relationship with the Swiss government was equally unsure. Although not formally recognized in the diplomatic lists, he was nevertheless received in the Foreign Office and admitted to the diplomatic receptions.

Yet another major Russian institution in Switzerland was the Agence de presse russe, which distributed news releases on Russian affairs for the Swiss press. Founded privately in 1916 by the liberal leader, P. N. Miliukov, the agency had remained under the direction of Vladimir Viktorov-Toporov, who, according to some, received support from American sources.

Paralleling the pressures exerted on Swiss affairs by the various foreign missions was a growing unrest among the Swiss Socialists. Angered by the rising cost of living and scornful of the Swiss government's efforts to minimize the significance of the scandal within the General Staff, the so-called "Colonels' Affair," the Socialists had begun questioning the role of the military in Swiss life. After antiwar socialists, meeting at Kiental in April 1916, had called for opposition to war credits in the belligerent states, Swiss radicals challenged Swiss "militarism."

In June 1917 the Swiss Socialist Party held a special conference in Bern to discuss the military question. Over the objections of many party veterans, the delegates voted to reject the principle of "defense of the country" (*Landesverteidigung*). In order to avoid a devastating party split, the assembly also adopted an amendment declaring that the Swiss party was ready "together with the socialists of all countries to give up the defense of the bourgeois fatherland." The amendment diluted the impact of the party's stand by putting it into the context of a general international movement, but the party had now made clear its challenge to the government and the policy of armed neutrality.[15]

The decision of the Bern conference represented the first major victory of the Zimmerwald Left, the Leninist wing of the Zimmerwald movement, in winning acceptance of its position by the Swiss Socialist Party. It also completed the process whereby Russian socialism replaced German socialism as the most influential foreign element in the development of Swiss socialist thought.[16] The debates within the party now tended to be conducted in the shadow of Lenin's "Theses on the Tasks of the Zimmerwald Left in Switzerland" written in 1916 but published only in 1918, and his "Farewell Address to the Swiss Workers" given on the eve of his departure for Russia in the spring of 1917.[17]

In this restructuring of Swiss socialist politics, the heart of the radical movement lay in Zurich, where Lenin had lived in 1916 and 1917. At the beginning of

1918, the most prominent radicals in Zurich were Fritz
Platten, a member of the federal legislature and a secretary of the Swiss Socialist Party, Ernst Nobs, editor of
the Zurich socialist newspaper *Volksrecht*, and Willi
Münzenberg, the head of the socialist youth organization, the Jungburschen.

Platten had first gone to Russia to participate in
the 1905 revolution and as a result had spent time in
prison in Riga; in 1915 he had been one of the original
members of the Left at the Zimmerwald conference. An
enthusiastic supporter of Trotsky as well as of Lenin,
Platten had aroused the Bolshevik leader's wrath at
times for his ideological vacillation, but he joined the
Bolshevik cause definitively when he prepared the way
for Lenin's fateful return through Germany. In January
1918 Platten was credited with saving Lenin's life in
Petrograd when the car in which the two were riding
was fired upon.[18]

Nobs had supported Lenin in 1916 but had opposed his intrigues within the Zurich party in January
1917. In later years he was to deny vehemently that he
had been a member of the Zimmerwald Left but in this
period he was commonly considered to belong to that
group. A close associate of Platten's, he treated the
Bolsheviks sympathetically in his newspaper.[19]

Willi Münzenberg had won considerable promi-
nence by his work in developing the Jungburschen into
a significant force in Swiss politics. To the disgust of
Orthodox Marxists, the Jungburschen had been strongly
influenced by Fritz Brupbacher, a well-known anarchist.
(At the beginning of 1918, Brupbacher, who was now
undergoing a conversion to Bolshevism, was remaining
uncharacteristically quiet.) According to Münzenberg, it
was once said of the Jungburschen, "We have members
in whom the drive for freedom has developed so far that
they even avoid lined paper in writing their thoughts so

that they don't let the lines bind them in a certain direction in writing."

The Jungburschen reveled in criticizing and mocking the leadership of the Swiss Socialist Party. Once when Hermann Greulich, the party's patriarch, shouted in anger at hecklers, "And if for nothing else I can expect respect for my gray hair," the answer came back, "I have never yet seen a donkey which had no gray hair."[20]

Behind the Jungburschen's lack of respect for their elders lay an intense desire for action; during the war this drive found its outlet in the foundation of an International Youth Secretariat in April 1915. This organization superseded the more passive International Youth Bureau which had earlier been centered in Vienna. Heading the Secretariat was Münzenberg, a native of Erfurt, Germany, who had come to Switzerland in July 1910, and had immediately joined Brupbacher's circle.

Under Münzenberg's leadership, Swiss youth groups developed a closer cooperation and grew in size, especially during the war. According to Münzenberg's own figures, the number of groups increased from three in 1906 to fifty-three in 1914 and 164 in March 1918 (including now fourteen French groups). The number of members stood at 180 in 1906, 944 in 1914, and 5,500 in January 1918. Münzenberg combined a concept of elitist leadership with his energy in winning members; the growth of the organization did not dilute its devotion to revolution.

From the very beginning of the war, the Jungburschen took an internationalist position, much in contrast to their elders, many of whom, being German or Austrian, returned to their native countries to answer the call to military service. The youths even mounted demonstrations at the train stations in protest against the departure of the foreign socialists.

Münzenberg first met Lenin at the Bern youth conference in 1915, but only after Lenin had moved to Zurich in 1916 did the Bolshevik leader establish significant and lasting relations with the Jungburschen. The differences to be resolved were great. The youths' anarchist spirit distressed Lenin, who hoped that they would outgrow it. Also, the Jungburschen had expressed their opposition to the war effort by refusing to serve in the Swiss army. Lenin considered such action useless and advocated that the youths should not only serve but should even agree to become officers. The revolution needed trained leadership.[21]

On August 1, 1916, the Swiss national holiday, the youths organized a street demonstration which ended in a clash with Zurich police: "That was the baptism of blood of the proletarian youth organization of Switzerland."[22] Two days later, over twenty thousand persons came back into the streets in sympathy with the Jungburschen, and the youths threatened new demonstrations for September 3. That day, however, passed quietly, as the Bundesrat debated Münzenberg's expulsion from the country.

The Swiss officials considered Münzenberg personally responsible for converting the Jungburschen "from an occasionally mutinying but not dangerous youth group of the party into the revolutionary vanguard of the workers." At the same time, the police did not consider him violent. In April 1917 a police report noted, "He has never invited acts of violence here; rather he has more often warned against them." A year later, another report characterized him as being "no revolutionary nature boy; he is a mixture of revolutionary and diplomat."[23]

By 1915, however, even Münzenberg felt rumblings of discontent at his leadership; as he had criticized the socialist leaders for their passivity, so too did he begin to hear criticisms of himself as not being revolutionary enough. The first challenge came from a group publishing a monthly organ, *Der Revoluzzer,* which took its name from Brupbacher. (Brupbacher himself now admittedly realized, at the age of forty, that he was no longer a youth: "Thus one worked together with these youths and yet was still isolated from them.") In Münzenberg's view, this group was too anarchistic, mouthing the slogans of the class struggle, but actually emphasizing "individual development" (*Einzelbildung*).[24]

A more serious challenge arose in 1917 as two young radicals, Jakob Herzog and Toni Waibel, turned on Münzenberg with complaints that he had attempted to restrain street demonstrations and other actions. Herzog, a Swiss by birth and a cabinet maker by trade, had worked for the youth organization in Berlin in 1915 and 1916 until deported from Germany for participating in a political demonstration. Upon his return to Zurich, he became Münzenberg's assistant and heir apparent. For Herzog, "action was an element of life." Lenin reportedly said of him that he was the type which the proletariat needed for the revolution.[25]   When he broke with Münzenberg, Herzog joined Waibel and Hans Itschner in founding a new journal, *Forderung,* and their new organization quickly made great inroads into Münzenberg's following.

In November 1917 demonstrations by a pacifist wing of the youth organization led to a series of conflicts with police, culminating on the night of November 17-18 in a full-scale insurrection in which three demonstrators and one policeman died. The Swiss authorities arrested the leaders of the Jungburschen, and on November 20 the Bundesrat decided to expel Münzenberg from the country. On March 1, 1918, the Bundesrat banned all the major revolutionary youth publications, including *Forderung.*

Münzenberg protested against his expulsion, claiming that sure imprisonment and possible death awaited
him in Germany. (In the spring of 1917 he had traveled
secretly through Germany to and from Stockholm.) The
Swiss authorities hesitated—partly because the Zurich
police did not consider Münzenberg directly responsible
for the violence of November—and in the meantime the
radicals in Zurich organized protest meetings in Münzenberg's honor.

In a major gathering held in Zurich on January 16,
1918, some two thousand participants first drove recognized police agents out of the hall and then adopted a
resolution to the effect that "Comrade Münzenberg has
only done that which is the duty of every convinced
Social Democrat." Thereafter the meeting almost broke
up as the speakers turned on each other. Nobs was
criticized as having been "cowardly" during the November troubles, and hecklers repeatedly interrupted his
efforts to justify himself. Another veteran youth radical,
Alfred Bucher, made the mistake of calling the Italians
in Zurich "backward," and he was whistled down. It
took a major effort by Rosa Grimm, Robert Grimm's
estranged wife, to bring order back to the gathering. [26]

Münzenberg's troubles with the federal authorities,
who eventually ordered him interned, forced him out of
any major public role in Switzerland in 1918, but his
shadow lay across much of the radical activity which
continued in Zurich. The Jungburschen, now directed
by Emil Arnold, were not so forceful as a group, but
from their ranks came many activists.

Of particular interest to Bolshevik organizers were
the Italians in Zurich, many of whom had or still belonged to the Jungburschen. Francesco Misiano, the
editor of the Zurich Italian newspaper *L'Avvenire del
Lavoratore*, received direct aid for his publication from
Balabanova and the I.S.C. Close to Misiano, who had

recently become secretary of the Italian Socialist Party of Switzerland, was Domenico Visani, the secretary of the metalworkers' union of the canton of Tessino.[27]

Another key Italian in Zurich was Gustavo Sacerdote, the Zurich correspondent of *Avanti* (Milan), who had lived in the same house as Balabanova in 1916. Sacerdote had demonstrated his loyalty to Lenin in his dispatches on the Bolshevik's departure from Switzerland in April 1917. In 1919 Sacerdote told Swiss authorities that he had never had any association with the Bolsheviks and that he had not spoken with Balabanova since 1916, but in a letter written on October 8, 1918, Sacerdote declared, "I want to work for the Bolsheviks . . . for our cause."[28]

The Swiss government watched the Italians in Zurich with considerable anxiety, and their fears seemed justified at the end of January 1918 when officials in Zurich came upon a cache of arms and literature supplied by the German consulate and destined for Italy. Besides the consideration of Swiss neutrality, there was the danger that the anarchists would turn their weapons against their hosts. The authorities were therefore all the more alarmed when a bomb was discovered at a Zurich railroad station in April.

In French Switzerland the major radical figure supporting the Bolsheviks was Henri Guilbeaux, who had come to Switzerland in 1915 after receiving a medical discharge from French military service. Born in Verviers, Belgium, he was a naturalized French citizen, and before the war he had made a name for himself by introducing German writers to the French reading public. An anarchist in his own political leanings, he worked enthusiastically with people of all shadings on the political left, and he acted as the correspondent in Switzerland of the Parisian antiwar group *La Vie Ouvrière*. In Geneva in

1916 he began publication of his own monthly review, *Demain*, which the French government immediately banned.

When he settled in Switzerland, Guilbeaux was still very much under the influence of the French pacifist writer, Romain Rolland. At Kiental he met Lenin, and he rallied to the banner of the Zimmerwald Left. When Lenin left for Russia, he named Guilbeaux the Bolsheviks' agent in Geneva and their link with French radicals. In *Demain* and also *La Nouvelle Internationale*, Guilbeaux published pro-Bolshevik literature, and through Balabanova in Stockholm, he sent news reports on French and Swiss affairs to *Pravda*, the Bolshevik organ in Petrograd. In turn, Balabanova sent him money to support his publishing efforts.[29]

Among the people Guilbeaux worked with was Jules Humbert-Droz. A Calvinist minister who had refused military duty in 1916 for pacifist reasons, Humbert-Droz came into contact with Russian politics as first Paul Biriukov, once Tolstoy's secretary, corresponded with him, and subsequently more revolutionary Russians, especially G. Ia. Sokolnikov, got in touch with him. Biriukov's positive reaction to the Bolshevik revolution influenced him strongly, and Humbert-Droz believed that the Bolshevik desire "to put an end to the war and to struggle against the capitalist regime" overwhelmed all doubt about the nature of their rule in Russia. Individual pacifistic moves were ineffective, he concluded, and therefore the revolutionary movement headed by the Bolsheviks conquered his own Tolstoyan inclinations. By the summer of 1918, when Guilbeaux introduced him to the Bolshevik diplomatic mission in Bern, Humbert-Droz had become a loyal supporter. Writing in *La Sentinelle* (La Chaux-de-Fonds) on August 20, 1918, he declared that he considered the Bolsheviks "to be the only ones of all the socialist parties who had taken up the true struggle, that of all the proletariats against all the bourgeoisies."[30]

The role of foreigners among the radicals did not pass unnoticed. The Swiss had always prided themselves on their maintenance of the right of asylum. One Swiss historian has labeled asylum "the noblest heritage of neutrality." At the beginning of the war, the *Neue Zürcher Zeitung* had spoken glowingly of the traditional right of asylum: "And hopefully our chroniclers will also have fine things to report about many an emigré of this world war," but by 1916 the same newspaper complained, "The canton of Zurich already has enough foreigners without papers." And again, "The flood of foreigners in Zurich has made disturbing progress in recent years."[31]

The foreign missions in Switzerland also took note of the foreigners among the radicals. A British intelligence report spoke of the Jungburschen as being mostly foreigners, "a number of idealists of little intellect and hooligans" led by Münzenberg and Misiano. In February 1918, a member of the British Foreign Office noted, "The Swiss authorities are much alarmed at the socialist propaganda being carried on in Switzerland by outcasts from every country who seek refuge on Swiss territory." The British, like the French, felt it necessary to offer the Swiss advice: "One is forced to the conclusion that the Swiss Government are badly served by their agents and that the Federal Council are as often as not enlightened by the foreign missions as to what is going on in this country."[32]

Unnerving to both the Bundesrat and the foreign missions alike was the formation of the Olten Aktionskomitee on February 4, 1918. A conference of representatives of the trade unions, of the Swiss Socialist Party, of the socialist representation in the national legislature, and of the party press, called at the instigation of Robert Grimm, demanded that the Bundesrat improve the conditions of the workers in Switzerland. The conference also warned Swiss workers "not to allow yourselves to be misused as a military tool against your own class interests." Particularly unsettling was the conference's mention of a general strike as a possible weapon against the government. To coordinate the interests of the working class, the conference established a seven member Aktionskomitee with Grimm as its president. [33]

As the committee embarked on its work, it assumed a conspiratorial character, preventing even the leadership of the Socialist Party from learning the details of its deliberations. This aroused the distrust of leading socialists, but Grimm nevertheless succeeded in establishing the committee as the spokesman for socialist and workers' opposition to the policies of the government.

Grimm, who took a hard line in opposing the government and who spoke freely of the necessity of resorting to a general strike, maintained a very ambiguous relationship with the Zimmerwald Left. With amazing resiliency he had returned from the scandal in 1917 to a position of leadership within the Swiss Socialist Party. Almost always personally at odds with Lenin, he repeatedly showed signs of reconciling his differences with the Bolsheviks. He was a man of undoubted administrative ability, but the question of the balance between revolutionary zeal and personal ambition in his politics has continually defied the efforts of historians to evaluate both his intentions and his motives. In the spring of 1918 he seemed very much the revolutionary zealot.

In view of the Entente diplomats, the Bundesrat reacted too feebly to the challenge posed by the committee. Colonel Pageot complained bitterly, "The Olten Aktionskomitee continues to take the attitude of a state within a state, and the Bundesrat consents to deal with it as one power to another."[34] Opponents of the committee even referred to it as the "Olten soviet."

Between the domestic unrest and the foreign intrigue, the Swiss government found the path of neutrality laden with pitfalls. It had to confirm that neutrality by giving evidence of its readiness to resist all foreign incursions, physical or spiritual, and yet the socialist opposition again and again challenged the government's independence, charging it at one time with subservience to Germany, another time with subservience to France. The socialists questioned the usefulness of the military establishment; neutrality, they declared, was an illusion. The government found its policies repeatedly put to a test.

3: THE FIRST EMISSARIES

The Allied and Associated Powers had chosen to withhold recognition of the Bolshevik regime, but at the same time to maintain their diplomatic representatives in Russia. Through unofficial agents they remained in touch with the Commissariat of Foreign Affairs, and for the time being the Soviet authorities seemed willing to tolerate this sort of arrangement with Russia's erstwhile allies while the talks with Germany at Brest-Litovsk went ahead. For the neutral states such as Switzerland the situation was more complicated.

When the Soviet government publicly discharged the entire diplomatic service of the old regime in December 1917, the Swiss government anxiously inquired of its legation in Petrograd as to whether Trotsky had made any demand for recognition. Furthermore, since Onu had been apparently recalled, was it Lenin's intention to send another representative to Switzerland? Minister Edouard Odier responded that the Soviet government had in fact not yet made any demand for recognition. Trotsky, however, had recently raised questions about the diplomatic immunity of the foreign representatives in Petrograd, and this might be a sign of something to come. It was probably not in Switzerland's interest to inquire about the matter because this might force the Swiss to make a decision before the Great Powers did. Since the Entente missions seemed ready to deal informally with the Bolsheviks, even giving a visa to the courier Holzmann, Odier considered it best to follow "this solution, however abnormal."[1]

The question of recognizing a revolutionary regime was of itself nothing new for the Swiss, but the eco-

nomic policies of the Soviet regime raised unprece-
dented problems which the Swiss could not immediately
resolve. As news came of the nationalization of the
banks and of the renunciation of Russian state debts,
the Swiss feared that recognizing the Soviet government
could even allow Soviet claims on the money and investments of individual Russians in Switzerland.[2] The government also had to protect the interests of Swiss who
held Russian state obligations, and it had to consider the
fate of Swiss investments in Russia—estimated at least at
500 million francs, much of which lay in the watch
industry and in the tramways of Petrograd—as well as
the safety of Swiss still resident in Russia, estimated in
1914 as some eight thousand.[3] In the face of these
considerations, the Swiss government, however much it
hesitated to recognize the Bolsheviks, tended to yield
when the Soviet government eventually initiated the
question of representation. At the same time, the Swiss
nervously watched the reactions of other states to the
same type of problems.

On December 30, 1917, the Soviet government
formally named Litvinov and Karpinsky as its representatives in London and Bern, respectively. The Soviet
radio carried the news of the appointments on January
1, but the host governments received official notification only several days later. On January 4, the Swiss
legation in Petrograd reported Karpinsky's appointment
as "Commissar": "The Deputy Commissar for Foreign
Affairs is concerned that this agent be formally recognized, and he has let us know that one will refuse to the
Swiss legation in Petrograd the privileges which are
refused to the Commissar in Switzerland, who is already
in our country." The British, Odier noted, seemed inclined to tolerate Litvinov under similar circumstances.[4]

The Allies had by this point entrapped themselves
by their own abnormal policy of maintaining their dip-

lomatic representatives in Petrograd and demanding protection from a government which they refused to recognize.[5] As the Bolsheviks now demanded the right to
place their own representatives in foreign capitals and,
moreover, the right to send couriers to these representatives, the Allied states found it necessary to make some
sort of concessions. The diplomats in Petrograd, ever
mindful of their own uncertain situation, tended to
endorse this policy.

In receiving Litvinov, the British Foreign Office
endured all the problems which later beset the Swiss,
although in many ways the two governments responded
very differently. Somewhat embarrassed by the fact that
it had once considered deporting Litvinov, the Foreign
Office sought to be conciliatory, but it refused to yield
to Litvinov's demands for de facto recognition.

Litvinov immediately challenged the authority of
the former Russian mission, now headed by Constantine
Nabokov, and through an emissary he demanded that
Nabokov turn over the mission's building as well as its
funds, ciphers, and archives. Simultaneously another
Bolshevik agent posed a similar demand to the Russian
consul general, A. M. Onu, a cousin of the representative
in Switzerland. Both Nabokov and Onu rejected the
demands, and the Bolsheviks withdrew.[6]

The Foreign Office had been gradually restricting
Nabokov's freedom of action, even depriving him of the
right to send ciphered telegrams to his colleagues in
other capitals, but it refused to intervene in the confron-
tation between Nabokov and Litvinov, asserting that
this was now a matter between two alien parties, neither
of whom had full diplomatic standing. The office, however, ordered Scotland Yard to provide protection for
Nabokov in the event Litvinov attempted to take the
mission by force. The question, the British declared, was
simply one of who was paying the rent for the building.

When Litvinov asked the British Post Office to send him all the mail addressed to the "Russian Ambassador," the Foreign Office directed that he should get only the mail addressed to him personally.[7]

The Foreign Office also refused to receive Litvinov in its corridors, but, concerned with Bolshevik recognition of its own unofficial emissary to Petrograd, Bruce Lockhart, the office won Litvinov's agreement to an arrangement whereby a British official, Rex Leeper, was assigned specifically to the task of meeting the Soviet envoy—often in a park or in a tea house—and forwarding his communications to the British government.[8]

Paramount in the British considerations was the desire to maintain its own mission in Petrograd. For fear of reprisals against Britons in Russia, the Foreign Office yielded successively to Litvinov's demands for the right to use his own cipher—although one Foreign Office wag noted, "M. Trotzky having renounced secret diplomacy, M. Litvinov might telegraph 'en clair' "—and to use sealed bags. The office finally drew the line, however, when it received word that the Bolsheviks intended to name a Consul General for India. Even the fear of reprisals was pushed aside, as the British refused to accredit him. The Bolsheviks chose not to press the point.

Litvinov complained regularly about delays in sending and receiving telegrams, about his second-class status in the Foreign Office: "However, like Mr. Trotsky, I do not attach much importance to matters of etiquette and unnecessary formalities, and it is a matter of indifference whether I am received at the Foreign Office or not." The British in turn charged the envoy with seditious propaganda among Russians serving in the armed forces of the western powers. Nevertheless, the maintenance of even informal contacts continued to be important to both sides, and for the time being London tolerated Litvinov while the Bolsheviks welcomed the arrival of Lockhart.

On July 4, 1918, in a speech to the Fifth Congress of Soviets, Chicherin indicated that the Bolsheviks were more or less satisfied with the British reception of Litvinov. "He was given," the Commissar noted, "the right of sending and receiving couriers and of using cipher. Nevertheless, the relationship of the British authorities toward him was in many ways far from suitable to the dignity of the Russian Republic."[9]

In Switzerland, Karpinsky received formal notification of his appointment on January 7, in the form of a telegram from Vorovsky in Stockholm. A longtime resident of Geneva, Karpinsky had of late been working closely with Guilbeaux, translating items for inclusion in *Demain*. Apart from his hesitation in 1914 to accept Lenin's defeatist position on the war, he had always been a trusted and loyal Bolshevik.

Karpinsky, however, had already made plans to leave Switzerland with a new trainload of Russians, scheduled to depart in January. In November he had closed his library. He issued only one official statement, repeating the formula contained in the terms of his appointment: "All officials of the legations and military missions as well as all those persons in the service of the Russian republic who are presently in Switzerland for official purposes are to deliver to Citizen Karpinsky all documents which he might demand at the earliest occasion and to give him the moneys which the respective persons have received from the Russian State Treasury. Any refusal of Karpinsky's instructions will be viewed as crime against the state." Having made this announcement, Karpinsky departed without having contacted the Swiss government.[10] The Bolshevik government itself probably did not know of his travel until he had arrived in Petrograd at the end of January; at that time, without any mention of Karpinsky, the government announced Zalkind's appointment as Soviet representative in Switzerland.

Since Zalkind's journey to Switzerland was to last over three months, the first official representative from Soviet Russia to arrive in Switzerland was Eduard Holzmann, who crossed from France into Geneva on February 12, 1918. Holzmann left Petrograd at the end of December, traveling as a diplomatic courier, and his was probably the most unusual journey made by any Soviet diplomatic agent in the first year of Bolshevik rule, as he traveled through Scandinavia, England, and France before reaching Switzerland.

Referring to Holzmann as the "first Trotsky messenger," the English, at Balfour's personal order, agreed not to search either his luggage or his person. London insisted that Trotsky had agreed that Soviet diplomatic couriers should depart immediately after fulfilling their mission, but at Litvinov's request, the Foreign Office agreed to permit Holzmann to remain a few days after his arrival on January 22. Diplomatic eyebrows raised a bit at reports that Holzmann intended to speak to trade union meetings, explaining Soviet policies, but the visit in fact passed without serious incident. Holzmann's mission in London seemed to involve bringing Litvinov his credentials and ciphers as well as investigating the general conditions of Russian emigrés in England. (To the distress of officials in Petrograd, both Litvinov and Vorovsky had devised their own ciphers).

On January 31 Holzmann departed London, and on February 3 he arrived at Le Havre, where French authorities proved to be not so hospitable as the English, searching him and warning him against untoward activities. In Paris Holzmann again met with Russians and also with French Socialists; there being no Soviet envoy in France as yet, he had no formal diplomatic tasks.

Holzmann knew both London and Paris well. Accounts of his background varied, but according to Swiss sources, Holzmann, who was born in Warsaw in 1882, had lived in western Europe, and primarily London, from 1910 to 1917. In May 1917 he had returned to Russia and had become a member of the Petrograd Soviet.[11]

Upon his arrival in Switzerland, Holzmann declared that although he traveled with a diplomatic passport, "I am not a diplomat." He had no intention of establishing contact with the Swiss government: "They ignore us, we also ignore them." He refused to give interviews to "bourgeois" journalists; he spoke only to correspondents of socialist newspapers.[12] The socialist and bourgeois press alike chose to label him a representative of the Soviet government, and Holzmann seemed inclined to assume that role when it seemed useful.

In Karpinsky's absence, Holzmann had no formal diplomatic tasks in Switzerland. He made no effort to meet officials of the Swiss government; he dealt mainly with local radicals and interned Russian soldiers. He apparently wanted to travel on to Italy, but Rome would have nothing to do with any Bolshevik emissaries. At the end of February he vainly sought a visa to travel back through France, and, failing this, he applied for a German visa. When the Germans delayed answering him, he found himself forced to stay in Switzerland far longer than he had intended.

Agents of both the Entente and the Central Powers watched Holzmann with great suspicion as each thought that he might be working for the other side. Partly because of this and partly because of the novelty of having an official Bolshevik agent in the land, the Swiss Political Department requested that the police watch Holzmann's activities carefully "but inconspicuously." As a result, it is possible to reconstruct his activities with considerable detail.[13]

Holzmann's work, while limited, offered an interesting example of how the revolutionary regime established its contacts abroad. He came to Switzerland ostensibly as just a courier, but he had a list of persons whom he was to see, and in turn leading radicals there had been notified by Balabanova and Vorovsky of his mission. He sent reports of his work to Stockholm for transmittal. The Swiss, however, probably overestimated his accomplishments. Having been sent forth from Russia at the end of December, he was clearly out of touch with more recent developments. He seemed to accomplish more in the way of identifying sympathizers than in organizing them.

Holzmann's first contact in Geneva was Guilbeaux. According to some Swiss reports, Guilbeaux met Holzmann at the train station—which would imply advance notification—but Guilbeaux later claimed that he had unexpectedly received a telephone call from the courier upon the latter's arrival in Geneva.[14] In the next two days, Holzmann also met local Russians, especially Anatole Divilkovsky, who was now working for Guilbeaux's *Demain*, and Abraham Shaikovich, a leader of radical Russian students in Geneva. He also spoke at length with Gustavo Sacerdote, who had come to Geneva just to see him.

Holzmann and Guilbeaux had much to discuss, as Holzmann brought news of the French government's intention to charge Guilbeaux with treason. Divilkovsky and Shaikovich introduced the courier to the affairs of the Russians in Switzerland. A number of Russians, moreover, simply came to him to inquire about personal problems, and Holzmann in turn sought out local prominent Russians. On the evening of February 15, he had his one meeting with Jacques Dicker, a Russian socialist emigré who had become a prominent figure in Geneva politics.

Through Divilkovsky, Holzmann established contact with Stefan Bratman, in Zurich, who now headed the Central Secretariat of Emigré Funds. When Bratman came to Geneva on February 17, however, he found that Holzmann had accepted an invitation to visit interned Russian soldiers in Yverdon, and after waiting vainly at Shaikovich's home, Bratman hurriedly returned to Zurich on the same day as he learned that Holzmann was traveling directly from Yverdon to Zurich.

Holzmann had originally been scheduled to address a gathering of Zimmerwaldists in Geneva on Monday, February 18, but on the sixteenth, after first having vainly asked Holzmann not to speak, the Geneva police had banned the meeting. The socialists had appealed the ruling, but the Great Council of Geneva upheld it. Although Geneva radicals met in any case, Holzmann was not present.

Zurich police later discovered that Holzmann had arrived in their city on February 17, but he had again checked out of his hotel on the morning of the eighteenth. His whereabouts that evening were unknown, although the police noted that the lights in Sacerdote's residence burned late into the night. On February 19, Holzmann again surfaced, checking into the Hotel Zentral in Zurich.[15] The local police attempted to establish surveillance on his activities, but their quarry immediately challenged his pursuer. As a result the Swiss authorities could renew their watch only on the twentieth. What they apparently missed were meetings between Holzmann and Platten, whom Divilkovsky had urged to meet Holzmann's train, Münzenberg, and Bratman.

Fritz Platten had himself just returned from Russia, where he had spent about a month.[16] He had traveled as the director of the train on which Karpinsky had left Switzerland, but although he had actively participated in the meetings of the foreign radicals in Petrograd, he had apparently heard nothing of Holzmann. In a cablegram to Vorovsky, Platten questioned, "Alleged Russian Holzmann presents himself here as envoy of the People's Commissars. Do you know him? Telegraph immediately." In a letter to Guilbeaux and Divilkovsky Platten asserted, "I have ground for suspicion that the man is in no way legitimized on the Russian side."[17] Platten's understanding of the diplomatic situation was that Divilkovsky was to be the Soviet representative in Bern, Guilbeaux the consul in Geneva, and his own wife, a Russian, the consul in Zurich. Platten's initial confusion would seem to confirm the view that, contrary to the thoughts of many Swiss, Holzmann had originally had no definite role to play in Switzerland.

The Zurich police observed Holzmann meeting mainly with Sacerdote, Bratman, and Max Horwitz-Walecki, a Polish socialist emigré.[18] On the evening of February 20, he addressed a gathering of some twenty Russians who "greeted him heartily." The following afternoon, he visited a group of Russian students who had sent him a telegram in Geneva saluting him as the "first delegate of the Russian proletarian government" and inviting him to speak to them.[19] Otherwise his activities consisted mainly in brief conversations and even windowshopping on the Bahnhofstrasse.

Holzmann's most suspicious activity came on the evening of February 21, as he left his hotel at 8:35: "It was striking how he walked up and down for a long time in the lonesome and dark Schützengasse and looked toward all directions." After some time he suddenly strode off quickly and met Bratman and two Russian women—probably Bratman's wife Maria and Sofia Dzerzhinskaia, the wife of the head of the Soviet political police—at the St. Annahof, where they immediately launched an intense conversation which lasted until the closing of the café at 11 o'clock. The next day Holzmann checked out of his hotel at 7 a.m. and returned to Geneva in the company of Platten. Guilbeaux met them at the station, and Platten returned to Zurich the same day.[20]

At this point, Holzmann apparently considered his work done. On February 22 he registered at the Hotel International in Geneva as being in transit from Zurich to Paris. On the whole, the evidence does not support the wide variety of claims bruited in the Swiss and the French press that Holzmann was possibly seeking to organize an international socialist conference or to urge the Swiss government to press for a general peace, or even to establish Bolshevik propaganda bureaus. His tasks seemed much more modest: to collect information on Russian emigré colonies and possibly on workers' movements in the Entente countries.

The French now refused him a visa to return through Paris. On January 17 Clemenceau's government had declared that it would receive no Bolshevik envoys, but French authorities had probably allowed Holzmann to pass because his destination was in fact Switzerland. Now they would not readmit him, even though the Swiss government expressed hopes that they would relieve the Swiss of their unwelcome guest.[21] Ironically, while some circles demanded that Holzmann be deported from the country, he himself found it impossible to leave.

Holzmann was visibly upset on February 23 when on the one hand Geneva authorities declared that they did not have his passport, and on the other, the French consulate declared that it could not deliver his visa. On February 25 he traveled to Bern, where, on the next day, he vainly went from the French mission to the federal police and again to the French mission. Although his passport finally turned up in the police station, a visa was still not to be had.

At this time, the Swiss authorities decided to terminate their close surveillance. Holzmann had become extremely suspicious and watchful: "Even while underway, he would often stop and look around, or else he would place himself in front of a business show window in order to observe his surroundings."[22] After remaining a few more days in Bern, now applying for a German visa, Holzmann retired to Zurich on March 2 and settled in a room on Riedtlistrasse. He still made some mysterious moves, but he often spent whole mornings simply reading in his room. He ate alone, and he rarely went out at night. He received little mail.

On March 22 Zurich police notified him that a Russian train was leaving the next day and that he should depart with it. He replied that much as he would like to, he could not do so on such short notice. He had checked luggage in Geneva and simply could not fetch it in time. Nevertheless, he promised the Swiss, he would continue to do whatever he could in order to return to Russia as soon as possible.[23] On April 2 he sent a telegram to Adolf Joffe, then preparing for Berlin, asking for help in obtaining a German visa; he had as yet received no answer to his application.

Despite his seeming life of a recluse and his obvious desire to return to Russia, Holzmann still maintained a degree of activity. On April 21 he asked Joffe for help in repatriating a group of 150 Russian emigrés, and Willi Münzenberg later declared that Holzmann had been the major source of information for him in writing his book, *Kampf und Sieg der Bolschewiki* (Zurich, 1918).[24] Now waiting for Zalkind, Holzmann acted as the major Soviet representative in Switzerland.

Zalkind's odyssey to Switzerland merits discussion for itself since it exemplified the dangers and problems of international travel in the first months of 1918. Zalkind left Petrograd on February 1, accompanied by Lev Kamenev, who had been named Soviet representative in Paris, Zalkind later characterized their task as being "to confront the Entente countries with the fact of the socialist revolution in Russia."[25] Writing in 1918 he described his work as being "in order, to represent the Soviet government in these countries, to give aid and protection to Russian citizens, and to struggle against the press campaign threatened by the press of Europe."[26]

From the first step Zalkind and Kamenev ran into problems. They could not pass through Torneo, Finland, which was held by the Finnish White Guard, and instead had to travel through Tammerfors, held by the Red Guard. Even there they had trouble because no one understood their documents: "But it sufficed that one pronounced the magic word 'Bolshevik' for all these difficulties to vanish in a stroke." Attaching themselves to a group of Swedish refugees, the two men then reached Stockholm on February 8, where they were welcomed by Vorovsky.

In Bergen, Norway, at the insistence of the British consul, they were held up for three days, waiting for formal acknowledgement to come from the French Foreign Ministry that they could indeed enter that country. Only with this certification would the consul allow them to proceed to Great Britain.[27] In Aberdeen, Scotland, despite their diplomatic passes, officials confiscated their luggage, books, and papers. The British authorities declared that these would be returned upon their departure from the country. "Without diplomatic valises and without money," they finally reached London, where Litvinov immediately took up their case with the Foreign Office, and members of the House of Commons questioned their government's actions.

The Swiss government had been watching Zalkind's progress with misgivings ever since its minister in Petrograd, on January 31, had announced Zalkind's nomination. The Bolsheviks had made no effort to obtain an agrément for this appointment, and in Odier's words, Zalkind, "Trotsky's special adjutant, is considered one of the most fanatical leaders of the Bolsheviks." The Swiss mission had given him a visa "without reservations" although it sought to make clear that "the visa in no way implies the recognition of Zalkind's diplomatic character." In a supplementary report two days later, Odier urged his government not to allow itself to be rushed "into a premature recognition." The Political Department should receive Zalkind, for fear of reprisals against the mission in Petrograd, in the same way that the Swedish government tolerated Vorovsky.[28]

In London, the Swiss minister requested the British government not to permit Zalkind and Kamenev to proceed. Eventually, when the French decided not to admit the two emissaries—this about the time that Holzmann failed to receive his visa in Geneva—the British ordered them out of the country. Litvinov protested angrily, but the French Ambassador, Paul Cambon, refused to receive the Russians. Litvinov charged that the British were "deliberately seeking to provoke a conflict," and he threatened to leave London together with Zalkind and Kamenev.[29]

The British nevertheless informed the two Russians that they had to be on the next boat leaving for Norway. In Aberdeen they received back the books, money, and valises except for one piece, Zalkind's, which had been left in London. They still had to experience "one last ignominy": they had to be deloused. Meanwhile, the Swiss hopefully speculated, "We may yet be spared the visit of this unusual envoy."[30]

By the time that Zalkind and Kamenev reached Christiania on March 8, the Bolsheviks had signed the Treaty of Brest-Litovsk. Kamenev chose to return to Russia, but Zalkind now sought a German visa. This also took time—seven weeks—and in the meantime Zalkind received his last valise back from the British. On April 30 he finally obtained a German visa.

Zalkind had requested permission to pass through Berlin, so as to confer with Joffe. But at the German frontier, Warnemünde, the German officials directed him to proceed directly to Switzerland without stopping. The Germans, too, were wary of the man. The German representative in Stockholm commented that Zalkind's manners "are said to be strikingly bad even for a Bolshevik." The Auswärtiges Amt had discussed the possibility of refusing passage to Zalkind, but when diplomatic relations between Germany and Soviet Russia became formalized as a result of the ratification of the Treaty of Brest-Litovsk, they had no reasonable excuse. In the end, Zalkind's perseverance paid off; on May 7 he arrived at Thayngen on the Swiss frontier—in his own words, "a pilgrimage of three months and one week in the service of the International."[31]

At every step along the way, Zalkind had complained bitterly at the treatment being accorded him, "an envoy of Russia"; he persistently argued, but in vain, that he should enjoy diplomatic immunity. In Switzerland, his friends, who had long expected him, hailed him as a representative of Soviet Russia, but, like Holzmann, he never presented his credentials to the Swiss government. Like Holzmann, his mission apparently had little to do with traditional diplomacy.

A French intelligence report, dated January 31, 1918, linked Zalkind and Platten as being charged with the task "to organize maximalist propaganda" in Switzerland. In his memoirs, Zalkind connected his own and Kamenev's missions with the news of "large scale unrest among workers and sailors in the countries of the Central Powers." In a letter to Guilbeaux, Balabanova spoke of Zalkind as having been "charged with organizing the publication of documents concerning the Russian revolution." Platten, she declared, would be able to explain.[32] The evidence points to Zalkind's mission as being concerned more with propaganda than diplomacy.

Upon Zalkind's arrival, Holzmann immediately summoned Guilbeaux to Zurich. On Sunday May 12, Holzmann met Guilbeaux at the Hauptbahnhof and accompanied him to Stefan Bratman's apartment, where Zalkind was waiting. Guilbeaux immediately took to the newcomer: "He did not lack spirit, he was interested in everything, and he could employ a ferocious irony." Zalkind, moreover, fearlessly discussed the mistakes of the Soviet regime, "as Lenin could do."[33]

In his memoirs of the meeting, Guilbeaux did not specify who was present in Bratman's apartment; he spoke only of "an Italian," probably Sacerdote or Misiano. Most likely Fritz Platten was also there. Although Guilbeaux also did not specify the subject of the meeting, the group probably exchanged information and spoke of organizational plans. On this occasion Zalkind told Guilbeaux that his salary as a *Pravda* correspondent was being raised from 300 francs per month to 500. (Zalkind apparently delivered a sizeable sum of back pay to him.)

At about this same time, yet another Soviet citizen drew the attention of western intelligence agents. Baruch Lipnitsky, born in Lida in 1876, had been a student at the University of Lausanne before the February Revolution. It is unclear whether he then left Switzerland and returned in May 1918 or whether the intelligence agents only noticed him now as he came into contact with Zalkind. In any case, he had received accreditation as a correspondent for *Pravda*, but Colonel Pageot insisted that this served only as a cover for his real mission, namely the task of establishing communications between pro-Zimmerwald groups in France, England, and Italy. An English report called Lipnitsky "Lenin's personal agent," charged with the task of effecting "the coalition of the Zimmerwaldist groups in Switzerland and the Entente countries." Pageot also claimed that Lipnitsky gave 2000 francs to Guilbeaux as subsidies for *Demain* and *La Nouvelle Internationale*. [34]

When Lipnitsky subsequently settled in Lausanne, the French became convinced that he was sending revolutionary propaganda into Italy. On June 23 he left Lausanne—the French thought for Lugano—and he dropped out of sight.

Zalkind and Holzmann remained in Zurich until the arrival of Jan Berzin, the new Soviet envoy named in April. (*La Nouvelle Internationale* wrote glowingly of Zalkind's altruism in voluntarily turning over the post of Plenipotentiary Representative to Berzin.) On May 21, the two men moved to Bern. The Swiss police thought that at first Berzin's entourage had reacted coldly to them, but very soon the two, although not officially members of the mission, were working closely with it.

Zalkind and Holzmann, despite their official diplomatic designations, had never made any effort to get in touch with the Swiss government. Through their preparatory efforts, however, the Berzin mission found a rather extensive network of agents, sympathizers, and informants awaiting it in Switzerland. The Bolshevik revolution held a great attraction for the radicals in Switzerland, and the Soviet diplomatic mission was accredited to them even more than it was accredited to the Swiss Federal Government.

4: THE STRUGGLE FOR RECOGNITION

The signing of the Treaty of Brest-Litovsk between Germany and Soviet Russia at the beginning of March opened new perspectives for Soviet foreign policy. Lenin's envoy to Berlin, Adolf A. Joffe, was accredited to the Imperial government, but his major task lay in encouraging revolution. At the same time, his presence, clothed in diplomatic immunity, provided a road to Switzerland and thereby to the continental Entente powers. Joffe now superseded Vorovsky as the channel of communications between Petrograd and Central and Western Europe.[1]

On April 17, to the surprise of the Swiss government which was still anxiously eyeing Zalkind in Scandinavia, the Russians announced that Jan Berzin had been named Plenipotentiary Representative in Bern. Since Zalkind had probably not been meant to be a diplomatic agent, this represented no contradiction in the minds of the Bolsheviks, but the move left the Swiss completely confused. On the other hand, the French refusal to receive Kamenev and the Italian hostility to Holzmann had made it all the more urgent for the Bolsheviks to establish themselves in Switzerland.

The Swiss consulate in Moscow promised to give Berzin a visa immediately, but it declared that the final permission to enter Switzerland would be granted only by the Swiss mission in Berlin. Because of the problems of communication between Moscow and Bern, this was a standard procedure; the Swiss representatives in Russia attempted to be as accommodating as possible, leaving final decisions to the mission in Berlin which could receive more detailed instructions from Bern.

Jan Antonovich Berzin, born in Latvia in 1881, had joined the Latvian Social Democrats in 1902, had participated in the revolution of 1905 in the Baltic area, and in 1907 had served as secretary of the Petersburg committee of the Russian Social Democratic Labor Party. An emigré from 1908, he steadfastly supported the Leninist wing of the party and played an important role in the Latvian party's decision, taken at its Brussels congress in 1913, to join the Bolsheviks. He represented the Latvian Social Democracy at the all-Russian unity conference in Brussels in mid-July 1914, at which time he supported the Bolshevik delegation in opposing the efforts of the other groups to censure Lenin.

In 1915 Berzin attended the Zimmerwald conference where he joined Lenin's Zimmerwald Left; in 1916 he traveled to the United States, returning to Russia after the February Revolution. On Lenin's orders, Berzin and Kamenev conducted the negotiations with the Left Socialist Revolutionaries on the formation of a coalition government after the October Revolution. Lenin and Krupskaya vacationed with him in Finland at the beginning of January 1918, and in February Berzin, together with Mark Natanson, a Socialist Revolutionary, was named a member of the abortive mission to establish a new propaganda organization in Western Europe. In short, Berzin had long been a trusted and loyal Bolshevik.[2]

Lenin, who had frequently shown great concern for the health of his followers, had selected Berzin for this position partly because of the latter's bad health at this time; a stay in the Swiss mountains should be beneficial. At the same time, however, Berzin's cultured manners, which stood in sharp contrast to Zalkind's curtness, seemed better suited for a formal diplomatic post. Berzin made an unfailingly good impression on the foreign diplomats with whom he had to deal.

Besides being confused by the mistaken rendering of the new envoy's name as "Janversine," the Swiss Foreign Office could not understand the relationship of this appointment to Zalkind's mission: "Since Herr Zalkind has already been announced to us in the same capacity, would we therefore have two Bolshevik envoys in Bern?" The government instructed its minister in Berlin, Dr. Philipp Mercier, to act "as cautiously as possible" toward both nominees.[3]

The confusion was subsequently resolved in Berlin by the intervention of Carl Vital Moor, a veteran Swiss Socialist who now played a peculiar role as a go-between for the German and Soviet governments. Eclipsed a decade earlier as a party leader by Robert Grimm, Moor had remained a member of the city council in Bern, and he had helped many Russian emigrés in Switzerland, including Lenin. In Russia during the winter of 1917-1918, he had come to Berlin in the company of Joffe.[4]

Moor sought out the Counselor of the Swiss legation, Dr. Karl Egger, and explained that the Soviet government had become dissatisfied with Zalkind's prolonged stay in Norway and had therefore chosen to send Berzin in his place. To Egger's dismay, Moor expressed his own personal regrets at this decision, "since he has known Zalkind for a long time as an extremely loyal comrade and a stirring agitator," but Moor also characterized Berzin as a "quiet, thoughtful, and very educated man." In Mercier's opinion, Berzin offered "a favorable exchange for us in every respect."[5]

The Political Department reacted positively to this report from Berlin, and on April 30 it notified Mercier, "We assume that the announcement of Janversine means the withdrawal of Zalkind's nomination. Under such circumstances we are no longer obligated to visa Zalkind's passport. Should Zalkind appear at the legation, we empower you to explain the situation to him."

Berzin should receive a regular, not a diplomatic, visa, and Mercier should assure him of a friendly reception in Switzerland.[6]

The Swiss government, however, quickly discovered that this problem could not be so simply resolved. On May 8 Mercier notified the Political Department that the Soviet mission in Berlin had presented him with seventeen passports for visas. All had received visas from the Swiss consulate in Moscow on May 1. Mercier asked for immediate instructions as to what he should do.

The Political Department had received no warning from Moscow that Berzin was bringing such an entourage with him. The government, moreover, found that it had no information at hand concerning the individuals named by Mercier, and, to complicate the situation still further, it now learned that Zalkind, whom the Germans had not permitted to visit Berlin, had just arrived in the country. For the moment, the Political Department did nothing.

In the next few days Mercier was able to offer more information. After meeting Berzin personally, the Swiss minister reported having "a favorable impression." Berzin, he noted, was "decorously and cleanly dressed, wore gloves, irreproachably clean linen, conducted himself thoroughly decorously and nicely, and generally struck me rather sympathetically." Berzin had assured Mercier "that he has no agitators among his collaborators. Political propaganda and mixing into the domestic affairs of Switzerland is not foreseen, rather only the renewal of diplomatic, commercial and financial relations." Berzin, however, rejected Mercier's suggestion that he travel alone to Bern to straighten things out.[7]

By this time, the Russians had become angry with Mercier's refusal to act. To help the Swiss to decide more quickly, Joffe, through Moor, let the Swiss legation know that Moscow viewed any restriction on Berzin and his entourage "as degrading humiliation." Berzin also considered the delay a personal affront, and he threatened simply to return home. Joffe, angered by some of Mercier's comments, warned that Berzin's return would lead to reprisals against the Swiss legation in Russia, and both Egger and Mercier were convinced that this represented no empty threat. (Joffe indeed did urge his government to expel the Swiss mission and consulates.)[8]

On May 14 the Bundesrat agreed to accept Berzin, although the question of formal recognition was to be left open. The Political Department accordingly notified Mercier to give visas to all Berzin's personnel unless he had definite cause to object to specific individuals. At the same time, Mercier was to emphasize again to Berzin "that we are taking note of his assurance to refrain from any political propaganda and that there are no agitators among his coworkers." When asked, Berzin willingly renewed these declarations, and Mercier reported that the mission would proceed immediately.[9]

Even so, the Swiss mission in Petrograd still reported a Soviet protest, "on the principle of reciprocity," against the delay in granting visas to Berzin's delegation. The Political Department responded that there would have been no trouble had Berzin presented the names properly. Ironically, at just this same time, Litvinov filed a complaint with the British government to the effect that the British had not given him enough time to seek information from Moscow concerning a mission for whom the Foreign Office had requested visas.[10]

The Swiss government ordered its border guards to receive the Russian mission, "which to be sure provisionally has no real diplomatic character, but still should be received with international courtesy." The Swiss had eighteen names on their list, but in fact only fifteen crossed into Basel on May 17. The group included Berzin, his wife Rosa and their daughter, Elizabeth Rivlina, Grigorii L. Shklovsky, Liubov Pokrovskaia (the wife of the Bolshevik historian M. N. Pokrovsky), Johann Ahre, Semion Popov, Albert Peterson, Nikolai Liubarsky, Peters Starke, Maurice Leiteisen, Ernst Ekke, Ernst Bahne, and Artur Akke. Of these, Rivlina, Pokrovskaia, and Leiteisen had been recommended for the mission by Lenin personally.[11]

Since the Russians had arrived at the very beginning of the long Pentecost weekend, Berzin was able to visit President Calonder only four days later, on Tuesday, May 21. Calonder received the envoy unofficially, noting that Switzerland was ready to take up de facto relations with the Soviet government but this did not constitute recognition. In this regard, Switzerland had to await the action of the belligerent Great Powers. Berzin in response again repeated his "formal assurance to abstain from all socialist propaganda in Switzerland." Berzin reported home that Calonder also agreed to end its relations with the old Tsarist legation.[12]

Calonder's reference to the necessity of deferring to the actions of the Great Powers stemmed from the obvious concern which the western powers were displaying in regard to the reception of this Bolshevik mission. In his first report to London on the matter, Sir Horace Rumbold insisted that the Germans had sponsored the Bolshevik mission and that Berzin was no more than a German agent. Calonder, he declared, had offered support to Berzin "on condition that the support thus offered should remain quite secret." All these facts, he argued, offered "clear proof of collusion between Germans and Bolsheviks."[13]

However unwillingly, the Swiss government found itself slowly advancing toward recognition, and indeed it almost immediately granted Berzin a more definite status than either Vorovsky enjoyed in Sweden or Litvinov in London. An inquiry by the Political Department showed that the Swedes had not granted Vorovsky official recognition—it had not even been requested— and the Swedish Foreign Minister had no direct contact with him.[14] On May 25, Shklovsky, Counsellor of the mission, visited the Foreign Office to obtain the necessary diplomatic identity cards and asked about the possibility of formal recognition. The Swiss official, Dr. Walter Thurnheer, Deputy Director of the Foreign Office, brushed the question aside with a statement that Switzerland looked on all new republics with sympathy but that it could take no action in this case.[15] On May 27 the Foreign Office notified the other departments of the Swiss government of Calonder's statement, and it informed the Swiss mission in Petrograd that the Swiss government was acting "in the interest of our nationals in Russia as well as of the Russians in Switzerland." Berzin had not requested recognition, and in any case, "under present circumstances" it could not be granted. The next day, the Bundesrat formally took note of the Political Department's intention to deal with the Soviet mission only verbally, not in writing, and it decided to leave the representation of Russia on the official diplomatic lists open and to call it vacant.[16] The Swiss hoped to avoid the necessity of choosing between Onu's legation and the new Soviet mission. Berzin, however, was unwilling to let the matter remain so uncertainly suspended.

As was to be expected, the Bolshevik mission received a mixed press in Switzerland. The pro-Entente Agence de presse russe issued "a protest to Swiss public opinion against the usurpers who claim to be the personification of the will of the Russian people." The socialist press, on the other hand, waxed enthusiastic.

The *Berner Tagwacht* fervently declared that every member of the mission was ideally suited for his assignment.[17]

Such commentary of course had little effect on Berzin, who immediately set about establishing the position of his mission. On May 25 he notified the Swiss Post Office of the presence of his mission and requested that all mail, telegrams, and money addressed simply to the "Russische Gesandtschaft" should be forwarded to Shklovsky, a former resident of Bern who had now reestablished himself at Falkenweg 9. (Shklovsky's wife and children had not accompanied him to Russia in 1917 and had remained at the old address.) The Post Office, noting that the Onu legation was still functioning, turned to the Political Department for advice. Before an answer could come, a larger crisis exploded.

On May 28, five members of the Bolshevik mission appeared at the building housing the Russian legation, located at Schwanengasse 4. When the Bolsheviks presented a letter asserting their right to the premises and its facilities and archives, Onu angrily declared his defiance of the revolution. Heated words followed, and Onu called for the police. (Onu had anticipated this problem and had asked the advice of Entente diplomats; the latter told him to resist and, if necessary, to call the police.)[18] When two policemen arrived, however, the altercation had ended; both Onu and the Bolsheviks had already departed the scene.[19]

Onu hastened to the Political Department, where he first sought out Gustave Ador and then Charles Paravicini, the Director of the Foreign Office. After excitedly relating the incident, Onu demanded the protection of the Swiss government, but Paravicini calmly replied that this was a matter between "two unrecognized legations." Perhaps Onu should seek the help of the Swiss police. The Russian vainly insisted on his right to protection, but Paravicini gave him no satisfaction.[20]

Up to this point, the Swiss government had generally followed the same course which the British government had followed when Litvinov had threatened to move against the old Russian mission in London. The British, however, had decided to protect those paying the rent on the building and had ordered Scotland Yard to prepare itself to evict any invaders. The Swiss acted in a more conciliatory fashion toward the Bolsheviks.

Practically on Onu's heels came Berzin, who also demanded the protection of the Swiss government. He asked Paravicini for a statement that he was the head of the "only Russian legation in Switzerland." Paravicini repeated the argument which he had given Onu, but Berzin was not so easily rebuffed. Should Swiss support be refused on grounds of nonrecognition, he declared, "then recognition will have to be demanded." In conclusion, Paravicini asked Berzin for a few days' patience. [21]

Among the Swiss themselves, confusion reigned. Bundesrat Müller, the head of the Police Department, questioned whether the Swiss government did not in fact have some obligation toward the Russian state which would necessitate action in regard to the archives. Both missions indeed had unofficial status, but the archives belonged to the Russian state. [22]

On May 29 Shklovsky came to the Foreign Office to complain that Onu had acted "rather uncivilly" toward the Bolsheviks, and he charged that Onu was at this point actually burning documents. The Swiss should act to prevent the destruction of the archives. Paravicini again responded that the Swiss had no role in this; Onu and Shklovsky should settle it between them. [23] Nevertheless, Shklovsky had emphasized just the point which was bothering Müller. (Shklovsky and Müller were neighbors.)

Immediately behind Shklovsky came Onu again, pleading for protection. Although he did not tell the Swiss, Onu had now begun preparing to shut down his mission. The French Ambassador had agreed to take the mission's archives to Paris under diplomatic pouch, and the British Ambassador had accepted "three small packets and a cash box" for safekeeping in the safe of the British legation.[24] Paravicini, on the other hand, now became convinced that Onu was destroying part of the archive.

The next day both Shklovsky and Onu appeared again to plead their cases to Paravicini. Shklovsky insisted that the matter was extremely urgent and could not be put off another day. Paravicini promised an answer by six that evening, and the Political Department sought to get in touch with President Calonder, who was out of town.[25]

At Müller's urging, Calonder sought the opinion of his legal expert; finally Calonder decided that the Swiss government should sequester the archives. Since neither he nor Müller, who was also Vice-President, were in Bern, he notified the Political Department of his decision by telephone, and it fell to Bundesrat Schulthess to act on behalf of the council and to order the Bundesanwaltschaft, the Federal Attorney-General, to protect the archives of the Russian legation from destruction.[26]

The Entente diplomats in Bern considered Müller and Schulthess to be the two members of the Bundesrat most sympathetic to the German cause. The British ambassador accordingly reported to London that since Müller seemed to be playing a leading role in the decision of the Swiss government, he "may be acting at the instigation of the German legation." British Foreign Office officials, upon reading this dispatch, expressed concern that the Germans would go on to employ the same maneuver in other neutral capitals, but Lord Hardinge took a more cautious view: "At first sight it strikes one as a highhanded proceeding, but the situation of Russian Missions is so abnormal that it is difficult to grasp the legal aspect of the situation."[27]

At 6 p.m. on May 30 Onu again came to Paravicini, who announced his government's decision to sequester the Russian legation's quarters and archives. Onu protested bitterly but promised that there would be no resistance. At 7 p.m. Paravicini notified Shklovsky of the decision, and at 7:15 the Swiss police arrived on Schwanengasse to carry out their task. In orderly fashion and with the cooperation of Onu's chief aide, the police went from room to room, making an inventory of the furniture, trunks, files, and chests, sealing each in turn.

The only serious challenge to the procedure came when the police reached the third floor of the building, which contained the offices of the Russian Military Attaché, General Golovan. Golovan insisted that his was a separate mission, sent by the Ministry of War and independent of the legation. Furthermore, he argued, most of the furniture and papers were his own personal property and not that of the Russian state. When the police called Paravicini for directions, the order came to seal the military attaché's offices too. When the task was completed, the police left behind a guard to protect the building.[28]

On May 31 Onu paid another visit to the Political Department, delivering a formal note of protest claiming that the Swiss action was a violation of extraterritoriality without precedent in international affairs. General Golovan also came in to demand the return of his private property, but he betrayed a feeling of defeat by asking whether he would still be permitted to reside in Switzerland. Paravicini assured him, "It goes without saying that all members of the former legation will be able to continue to reside in Switzerland as non-official persons."[29] On June 20 Golovan returned with the claim that since the files of the commercial attaché, housed in another building, had not been sealed, his should be released. Paravicini, however, stood firm, and Golovan admitted defeat.[30]

The Bolsheviks claimed a victory when the archives were sealed, declaring that the Swiss government had responded to their demands. The Political Department attempted to argue that it had acted impartially solely to protect the diplomatic property of a foreign power,[31] but the course of events clearly favored the Bolsheviks for the moment. The fact of even a provisional recognition had been Onu's last weapon, and his legation now dissolved. Its members scattered around Switzerland in much the same fashion as had the personnel of the Bakherakht-Bibikov mission before it. On June 10, the Bolsheviks announced that their mission now represented the Russians in Switzerland, especially the interned soldiers, and they invited their compatriots to apply to Shklovsky at Falkenweg 9, which for the moment served as the mission's headquarters.

The Swiss Political Department nevertheless refused to grant full recognition to the Bolshevik mission and it made clear that it would deliver the archives only to the representatives of a de jure Russian government. On June 7, it directed the Swiss Nationalbank and the Kantonalbank to seal the safety deposit boxes rented by Onu's legation. The Nationalbank reported that the legation had a balance of some 45,000 Swiss francs. On the other hand, the Political Department found itself inundated with the unpaid bills of the legation, mostly for clothes and shoes for interned soldiers.

On May 31 the Bundesrat endorsed the action of sequestration, and on June 3 the Foreign Affairs Delegation of the Bundesrat considered the new situation. It simply took note of Onu's protests, and it put off consideration of a request by Berzin that the archives of the Russian consulates in Switzerland be similarly seized. The legation, the Delegation ruled, had now lost its diplomatic privileges. As far as the question of mail was concerned, all letters received between May 30 and

June 15, addressed to individuals, would be delivered as
indicated; those addressed simply to "Russische Gesandtschaft" or "Kanzlei der russischen Gesandtschaft" would
be returned to the sender with a request for more
specific information. After June 15, all mail addressed
to the Russian Mission or Legation would automatically
go to the Bolshevik mission.

Having failed to gain control of the archives by
direct means, the Bolsheviks attempted to employ indirect methods to the same end. A Bern attorney, Boris
Lifschitz, came to the Political Department to complain
in the name of the owner of the building on the
Schwanengasse that the sequestration prevented him
from renting the premises to anyone else. After some
deliberation, the Swiss, while noting that Onu had prepaid the rent until the end of June, decided that they
had best removed the sealed goods.

On June 10, when Swiss officials appeared at the
building to begin the process of moving, Lifschitz again
appeared, objecting in the name of the landlord, that
the removal of the furniture would undermine claims
against the legation. The Swiss ignored him, but in July
Lifschitz, who was working closely with Shklovsky,
returned to the Political Department as the representative of a variety of claimants against the legation; he
even brought the Bern Betreibungsamt, an official debt
collection agency, into the picture; but the Political
Department steadfastly refused to entertain claims
against a foreign government, and specifically against
the goods of the legation.

The job of packing and moving the contents of the
legation lasted five days, being completed only in the
evening of June 14. The archives and furniture eventually turned out to be something of an albatross for the
Swiss government; over the next two decades they had
to be moved several times because of problems of space

in government buildings. In 1923, moreover, the banks won the agreement of the government to emptying the safety deposit boxes which had been sealed. Only in 1946, after World War II, did the Swiss finally deliver the archives to the Soviet government.

At the time of the sequestration, several Swiss sources speculated that the action, which indeed seemed to be without precedent, would become a classic case in international law. The official explanation and justification offered by the Swiss government, contained in a legal opinion of August 5, 1918, argued that the Political Department had acted only to conserve Russian state property. Under normal circumstances, the host government had to recognize the inviolability of the archives of a foreign legation. The host government, however, could be held responsible for damage to such archives as a result of "illegal deeds of persons outside of the legation." In the case of uncertainty as to recognition, the host government can seal the archives just as it could in case of there being no representative as a result of an unexpected death: "The sequestration is in this case the type of interference which combines a minimum of violation of secrecy with the greatest measure of inviolability."[32]

The Entente representatives disapproved entirely of the Swiss action; Rumbold declared that the Swiss had played into the hands of the Bolsheviks and that they were obviously acting under German pressure. In considering Rumbold's statements, the British Foreign Office opined that the major obligation of a host government was not to touch the archives of a foreign legation. The British considered the Swiss concern that Onu would destroy the archives to be totally unfounded; Onu had specifically denied any such intention. In conclusion, the Foreign Office notified Rumbold that it considered the Swiss action of sequestration unjustified: "This expression of opinion is however for your information only, as it is not a case in which His Majesty's Government can take any action."[33]

At any rate, even though they failed to gain possession of the archives, the Bolsheviks had achieved a major victory in displacing the Onu legation and even depriving it of its furniture. By dispossessing Onu, the Swiss officials had indirectly recognized the Bolsheviks' superior position. On June 21, in a move designed to emphasize the mission's claim to being the legal heir of all previous Russian agencies in Switzerland, the mission moved into the house on Schwanengasse, enjoying for a few days the rent which Onu had prepaid.

The sequestration pertained only to the archives of the legation. The Bundesrat had refused to consider Berzin's request for the sequestration of consular archives. On June 20, a delegation headed by Zalkind attempted to take control of the Russian consulate in Geneva, but here they faced a more formidable opponent in the person of Gornostaev, who forcefully rejected the Bolsheviks' demands for the archives, keys, and money of his office. When Shklovsky came to Paravicini on June 21 to complain, the Swiss refused to act, insisting that consular archives did not constitute state property. Paravicini advised the Bolsheviks to seek civil action in the courts.[34]

On September 4 the Soviet government officially protested to the Swiss government against Gornostaev's refusal to surrender the consulate. The Swiss authorities, the Bolsheviks charged, had to bear full responsibility for tolerating this "institution, which employs a false name and insignia."[35] Nevertheless, Gornostaev for the time being remained at his post with his office intact.

Yet another point of contention in diplomatic practice came in the problem of establishing a courier service between Moscow and Bern. Normal diplomatic practice distinguished between regular and occasional couriers; the Russians ignored this distinction. The Swiss consul in Moscow, as noted above, gave visas on demand, with the understanding that the Swiss representative in Berlin would give the formal permission to enter Switzerland. Under these circumstances, Berlin soon became the battleground between the casual practices of the Russians and the meticulousness of the Swiss in the recognition of couriers.

All the western countries looked with suspicion at the pouches of the diplomatic couriers of the Soviet government, wondering what they contained. In the case of the courier service to Switzerland, however, there were more specific grounds for suspicions. Five members of Berzin's original entourage had been designated as couriers. On May 14 three more couriers presented themselves in Moscow for visas, another three on May 30, two on May 31, and five more in the first three weeks of June. (This seems to have been a significantly heavier traffic than traveled from Moscow to London.) The Swiss consul, Friedrich Suter, issued all these visas without question. In June the Swiss mission in Berlin, noting that not one of these couriers had yet made the return trip from Switzerland, decided to challenge some of the more dubious couriers.

Minister Mercier had suspected from the beginning that Berzin was to some degree subordinated to Joffe, and he became more convinced of this when Joffe proposed to send his own courier to Berzin. On June 13, the Swiss mission refused to grant this courier a visa, insisting that it could accept only "sealed official documents" being carried from the Commissariat of Foreign Affairs in Moscow. The Russian mission then telephoned for further explanation, and, dissatisfied with the answer, Joffe demanded a personal conference. Still angered by the delay of the Swiss in accepting Berzin—

"an incomprehensible, unfriendly act"—Joffe accused the Swiss mission of "personal chicanery against him and against the new Russian government." When the Swiss insisted that they could not accept couriers from one legation to another, Joffe still insisted on being granted an exception; Moscow counted on him to handle a large part of the business with Berzin. As Mercier summarized it, "He notes here the reports, etc., and then sends them on to Bern. The suspicion, already expressed earlier, that Mr. Berzin is in a certain way subordinated to Mr. Joffe seems to be only confirmed by this."

Joffe threatened retaliatory measures not just against Swiss couriers but also again against all Swiss in Russia. At the same time, in a more conciliatory gesture, he offered the Swiss the use of his own newly established direct wire to Moscow. Mercier turned to his government for instructions.[36]

Simultaneously, another controversy arose as Mercier hesitated to grant visas to two seemingly elderly couriers from Moscow. Mark Natanson, sixty-seven, the Left Socialist Revolutionary leader who had been named with Berzin to the abortive propaganda mission in February, and his wife, sixty-five, had both been among the first couriers named in May. Natanson reportedly carried six packages and his wife three; both bore the title "Permanent Diplomatic Courier." On June 22, the Soviet mission called for an explanation of the delay in granting the visas, and Joffe entered into an argument with Karl Egger which covered the whole spectrum of problems surrounding the sending of couriers to Switzerland.

Egger opened by noting that the German stamp in Natanson's passport indicated that he could not reenter Germany from Switzerland. That, in addition to his age, indicated that Natanson could not be a permanent courier. Furthermore, Egger questioned, why was the traffic only in one direction, into Switzerland? Why had Berzin not yet sent any couriers on the return trip? The indications were that the Natansons were being sent to Switzerland to stay.

Joffe responded in what the Swiss considered an undiplomatic tone. The Swiss had no right, he declared, to judge the quality and number of couriers which the Russians chose to send. Moscow could send one every day if it so wished, and the Swiss had no right to object. In the next breath, however, he admitted that Berzin had not yet sent a single message to Moscow. Possibly referring to Holzmann's unsuccessful efforts to persuade the Swiss to allow him to carry a diplomatic pouch, Joffe insisted that the Swiss were preventing Berzin from sending couriers and were generally harassing him.

When Egger countered with his suspicion that the Russians were simply helping Natanson reach Switzerland where he would leave the service—and this proved eventually to be the case—Joffe again threatened reprisals against Swiss couriers and citizens in Russia. Mercier then again appealed to his government for instructions, urging that the matter be discussed with Berzin himself.[37]

On June 23 Joffe telegraphed Berzin to complain about the Natanson case and to urge his colleague to make the Swiss aware that all these petty formalities were hindering relations between the two governments. Again threatening Swiss citizens in Russia, he instructed Berzin to demand a visa for Natanson. On the other hand, he reported that Moscow was dissatisfied with the lack of news from Switzerland: "Necessary to learn completely your situation Switzerland." Two days later Joffe again complained to Berzin about his poor relations with Mercier and Egger.[38]

Moscow's complaints about Berzin's silence were

coming from Lenin himself. In a letter of June 18 to Joffe, Lenin wrote, "I am extremely surprised and disturbed by the lack of news from Switzerland. They say that there are weekly couriers there. And not a word! What are Berzin and Shklovsky doing? Send them this letter please and take measures for obtaining an answer."[39]

On June 25 Berzin discussed the courier problem with President Calonder and apparently accepted the explanation that the Swiss would not grant an exception to the principle of accepting diplomatic couriers traveling only from the Foreign Ministry to a legation and not between legations.[40] On the other hand, Paravicini ordered Mercier to grant the Natansons their visas "as an exception." Hopefully, he stated, Joffe would now calm down. The mission was hereafter to let all couriers from Moscow to Bern pass "without reference to age, number, etc."[41]

Mercier still raised objections, pointing out that it would be a simple matter for Joffe to obtain a seal like that of the Commissariat of Foreign Affairs. To block the sending of packages from Berlin to Bern it might be necessary to require that the consul enter the number of packages into his visa stamp. Bern, however, instructed its minister that while he was basically right, "we wish, for reasons that you easily understand, to show a certain good will toward the Bolshevik authorities who generally seem rather well disposed toward our compatriots in Russia." The minister, in short, should be "conciliatory" toward Joffe. Mercier responded that he was now certain that Berzin "is simply an organ of Mr. Joffe." [42]

Chicherin would yet complain to the Fifth Congress of Soviets that the Swiss "are still sometimes making difficulties in admitting our couriers into Switzerland,"[43] but the question was essentially settled by the end of June. On June 27, moreover, Shklovsky reached agreement with the German mission in Bern on allowing Soviet couriers to travel back to Russia without interruption. The Germans had blocked Holzmann's departure from Switzerland, and this impasse had apparently contributed greatly to Berzin's failure to send other couriers home.[44]

The settlement of the courier question followed by a week the Bolsheviks' occupation of the quarter on the Schwanengasse. Berzin's mission was now as firmly established as it was ever to be; the Swiss, while not altogether satisfying Berzin and certainly antagonizing Joffe, had been forced into a number of concessions which they had not originally planned to make. They stopped short of recognition, but Berzin could nevertheless claim significant victories. Most important, Berzin's successes established a solid basis for the mission's activity in Switzerland.

5: DIPLOMACY AND PARADIPLOMACY

The Soviet mission differed sharply in character from the other diplomatic missions in Bern. For one, the Soviet mission had no military attaché engaged in intelligence operations. Instead, its information agencies collected reports on workers' movements in various European countries. On the other hand, like any diplomatic mission, the Bolsheviks vigorously attempted to influence the Swiss public opinion. They used direct means, such as the interviews with Berzin published in socialist newspapers throughout the country at the end of June, and also indirect means, such as offering funds to sympathetic publications. In addition, however, the Bolsheviks exploited their diplomatic status to disseminate revolutionary propaganda both in Switzerland and abroad.

In an effort to establish his position in the Bern diplomatic community, Berzin made the rounds of the foreign missions on June 1, leaving his calling card at each. Both the American and the British envoys were at first inclined to give their personal cards in response, and on June 2 the Entente representatives tentatively approved this idea. London agreed, but when Washington, Paris, and Rome all expressed disapproval of any contact with Berzin, the British joined in ignoring the Bolshevik mission.[1]

In August, Berzin used the expedient of the Swiss post in sending some dispatches to the American envoy, since he would not be received at the mission. Stovall duly forwarded the documents to Washington, noting, "I have not acknowledged this communication from the

Soviet representatives," and the Department of State approved his silence.[2] By way of contrast to the reaction of the Entente representatives, the representatives of the Central Powers gave Berzin their cards and exchanged visits. After meeting Berzin, the Austrian ambassador excitedly reported home, "Today for the first time in my life I have seen a real Bolshevik face to face."[3]

Russian citizens in Switzerland represented an obvious, legitimate area of activity by any Russian diplomatic mission. From the beginning of the war, the Russians had suffered great financial difficulties, and in the winter of 1917-1918 these had become still worse. On January 11, 1918, President Calonder received a delegation of Russian intellectuals who requested the Swiss government's aid in obtaining credit for their compatriots.[4] The relations between the political emigrés and the Tsarist mission had of course been strained, and under Onu the mission had still offered no relief. Upon its arrival, the Bolshevik mission met with hostility from both the monarchist and the liberal republican elements, but it enjoyed an enthusiastic reception from the radicals. After years of political exile, many Russians welcomed the advent of a mission from the homeland which cared for them.

The Agence de presse russe, as noted above, distributed protests by various organizations against the presence of the Bolsheviks. At the end of June, Russian student groups in Bern, Basel, and Zurich announced their secession from the Association generale economique des étudiants en Suisse, which had established contact with the Bolsheviks. On July 1 an assembly of delegates comprising L'Union provisoire des organisations des democrats et des socialistes russes en Suisse publicly proclaimed its allegiance to Kerensky, the man whom the Bolsheviks had overthrown.[5]

At the same time, the monarchists had also not yet given up hope. In a memorandum of May 4, Onu had warned the Entente powers of "a group of bankers, internationalists, for the most part Jews," which seemed to be taking German money. Onu identified Bibikov as a major figure, and he also named Vsevolod Sviatkovsky, once a Tsarist intelligence agent in Switzerland, who in 1917 seemed to have joined the Austrian camp.

The readiness of the Allied diplomats to identify every unsympathetic movement as pro-German had built-in contradictions which they ignored. In one breath, for instance, the British mission could claim that Sviatkovsky was pro-Austrian, and in the next it could report that Sviatkovsky, who was a friend of Wickham Steed, the editor of the London *Times*, had broken with Bibikov because the latter was a German agent. (The Austrians considered Sviatkovsky pro-French.)[6] The British mission, however, chose to shy away from the monarchists. When the League for the Restoration of the Russian Empire approached the British for their reaction to a proposed plot with the Germans to rescue the Tsar from Bolshevik captivity, the Foreign Office declared, "It hardly seems necessary or wise for the moment to give assurances or enter into relations with agents of Russian political parties in Switzerland." The Foreign Office preferred to rely on Bruce Lockhart in Moscow for its contacts with Russian groups.[7]

From among those contending Russian groups, the Bolsheviks worked with the radicals. Stefan Bratman, who had been one of the first emigrés to confer with Holzmann and at whose apartment Guilbeaux had met Zalkind, was the chairman of the Central Secretariat of Russian Emigré Funds, an organization which claimed to represent all the Russian political emigrés in Switzerland. At the beginning of July he moved from Zurich to Bern to work for Berzin, acting first as a specialist on

affairs of Russians in Switzerland and subsequently as
the commercial attaché of the mission. An engineer by
training, he had worked for several major Swiss firms.
His wife Maria took a position with the Soviet Red
Cross mission in Switzerland, handling correspondence
with interned Russian soldiers.

Another of Holzmann's early contacts, Maximilian
Rivosh, served as the mission's channel for dealing with
Russian student associations in Switzerland. Although
he never held an official post, he became virtually a
Soviet consul in Zurich. As president of a student
mutual assistance organization, he took money from the
mission for redistribution among the membership. In so
doing, he made clear that politics had to be a major
criterion for financial assistance—he even distributed
questionnaires among students concerning their attitudes toward the Soviet government. At one point,
Rivosh warned a comrade in Lausanne, "I recommend
that you consider that continued reports to the mission
about excessive granting of aid to 'doubtful' elements
can have the most unpleasant consequences for all
needy students." In particular, Rivosh named one student who was to receive nothing, since the mission
might otherwise react "in a most unpleasant fashion."[8]

Rivosh was himself a student in history at Zurich
university. In 1917 he began work on his doctoral
dissertation about the Russian Decembrists, but now he
had to devote full time to his work for the Soviet
mission. In October 1918, he complained, "Recently I
have been completely deprived of the opportunity to
study, and I am preparing to sit down to my work just
as soon as the train, of which I am one of the organizers,
leaves for Russia."[9]

The Bolsheviks' major agent among the students in
French Switzerland was Morduch Ganchak, a student in
medicine at the University of Lausanne since 1913. Up

to the time of the Bolshevik revolution, the Swiss police
had recorded no complaints against him, but in 1918 he
emerged as a local Bolshevik leader, maintaining con-
tacts with, among others, Guilbeaux, Rivosh, Romain
Rolland, Humbert-Droz, and Platten.[10]
The mission also recruited personnel from among
former Tsarist officials, a major example being Iurii
Iakovlevich Soloviev, who had come to Switzerland in
February 1918 from his last diplomatic post in Madrid.
At that time, insisting that he was sympathetic to the
Germans, he sought permission from the German mission to return to his estate in German-occupied Poland.
Although his request was denied, he did receive some
income from the estate. When the Soviet mission
opened, he approached Berzin declaring himself ready
to enter the Bolshevik service. The Soviet envoy replied
that men of Soloviev's experience "were always welcome even if they do not fully agree in their political
orientation with the goals of the present government."
Soloviev then began to work with the mission, helping
impecunious Russians in Switzerland, while at the same
time he told Baron Romberg that he personally favored
a reestablishment of the monarchy in Russia. Eventually, in November 1918, he left Bern for Petrograd, and in
subsequent years he worked in the Soviet foreign service.[11]
   In the uncertain area of activity between the interests of the Bolshevik party and of the Soviet state, the
mission also sought to establish relations with organizations and parties in Switzerland and the Entente countries. The mission formally extended invitations to Swiss
unions to send representatives, at the expense of the
Bolshevik government, to study the situation in Russia
for themselves. Through Henri Guilbeaux, the mission
sought to make contact with the French Confédération
Générale du Travail.

By way of contrast to these activities, the establishment of the Soviet diplomatic mission actually had little
effect on the course of relations between the Soviet and
the Swiss governments—apart perhaps from that of
avoiding an outright rift. The attitudes of both governments were conditioned primarily by other international
forces, especially by the decision of the Entente to
intervene militarily in Russia; Soviet-Swiss relations
went on in the shadow of general developments brought
about by European war and revolution.

Swiss interests in Russia concerned first of all the
fate of Swiss citizens and investments in that country.
In 1917 the Provisional Government had abrogated the
existing treaty on trade and on the treatment of each
other's nationals, which had been in effect since 1872.
The treaty was thereby due to run out in the fall of
1918, and as yet no move had been made to provide
new arrangements. The Swiss, who had themselves
stirred an international crisis with the nationalization of
their railways at the beginning of the century, also
looked anxiously at the Bolsheviks' program for nation-
alizing the Russian economy.

The specific diplomatic interests in Switzerland of
the Soviet government concerned the return of interned
Russian soldiers who had escaped from prisoner of war
camps in Germany or Austria and of those soldiers who
had deserted from the Russian expeditionary forces in
France. As the center of numerous international organizations, such as the International Red Cross, Switzerland also represented an important base for humanitar-
ian activities.

Over these specific interests on both sides lay the
international developments. The Soviet government was
concerned with maintaining its very existence in the
face of the Entente intervention. On May 25 fighting
broke out along the Trans-Siberian railroad, and as a

large scale Civil War developed in Russia, the Allies, who already had troops in Murmansk, Archangel, and Vladivostok, sent new forces in to fight on the side of the Bolsheviks' opponents. The assassination of the German ambassador in Moscow on July 6 further complicated the uncertain position of the Soviet regime. The Bolsheviks blamed the murder, actually carried out by Left Socialist Revolutionaries, on Anglo-French intrigue.

At the end of July the Allied diplomats, having moved to Vologda rather than accompanying the Bolshevik government to Moscow, chose finally to leave Soviet Russia altogether. The tenuous diplomatic relations existing since the October Revolution thereby received another great blow. Only skeleton staffs remained to man the former embassy buildings in Petrograd, while consuls and unofficial agents such as Lockhart continued to work in Moscow.

The Swiss government contained few if any enthusiasts for the Bolsheviks' style of government, and it had a number of officials who both supported the Entente's intervention and feared the Bolsheviks' efforts to encourage revolutionary movements. For the moment the Swiss refused to withdraw their embassy from Russia, but neither did they dare take any initiative friendly toward the Soviet government.

In this maze of contradictory and conflicting interests, neither the Swiss mission in Russia nor the Soviet mission in Bern served as a focus of relations between the two governments. As might be expected under the circumstances, a variety of go-betweens, private individuals, also carried messages, and the most intriguing of these was Carl Moor.

In years past, Moor, a member of the Great Council of the Canton of Bern, had helped Russian emigrés in Switzerland in a number of practical matters, including giving them money.[12] In the spring of 1917 he undertook two missions to Italy, apparently at the behest of the German mission in Bern. Subsequently, after Italian authorities had banned him from reentering the country, he expanded his activity to Scandinavia. He reported to the Austrian mission as well as to Romberg, although neither knew of his work with the other; because of his openly expressed sympathies for the cause of the Central Powers, both legations considered him a desirable alternative to his old rival, Grimm, in the camp of internationalist socialists.

Moor had participated in the Zimmerwald conference but not the one at Kiental. He had played no significant role in the Zimmerwald movement before 1917, but many suspected him of informing both German diplomats and also German socialists about developments in the movement. Because of this reputation, the Swiss Socialist Party in 1917 refused to name him its representative to a planned socialist conference in Stockholm.[13]

Grimm's disgrace in Petrograd offered Moor a new opportunity. Denouncing Grimm's behavior as "worthless, cowardly and slanderous," he joined the committee established by the I.S.C. in Stockholm to investigate the affair. Although, for some reason, Moor did not sign the final report, his relationship with the I.S.C. and with Balabanova now developed rapidly in the wake of Grimm's departure from the scene. He also began to work with Karl Radek and Jakob Hanecki, then the Bolshevik representatives in Stockholm.

Lenin had known Moor for a number of years, and in the years before the war Moor had apparently performed useful services for Shklovsky, then a student at the University of Bern, who was acting as Lenin's agent in some delicate money matters.[14] Nevertheless, in August 1917, Lenin, upon receiving reports about Moor, urged caution on Radek and Hanecki: "Incidentally, I do not remember who reported that apparently after Grimm, and independently of him, Moor showed up in Stockholm. That that scoundrel Grimm, as a centrist-Kautskyite, was capable of a base rapprochement with 'his' minister does not surprise me; whoever does not split decisively with the social-chauvinists, he always runs the risk of falling to this base position. But what kind of man is Moor? Is it completely and absolutely proven that he is an honest man? that he has never had and now has not either direct or indirect sniffing around [*sniukhivaniia*] with the German social-imperialists?"[15]

The Bolshevik Party rejected an offer of money from Moor at this time, but he continued to draw closer to Lenin's group. Probably their common antagonism to Grimm represented the most immediate bond, but, after first seeking contact with the Bolsheviks as part of his work on behalf of the Germans, Moor underwent a conversion to the cause of world revolution as interpreted by Lenin.

The Bolshevik seizure of power in November found Moor back in Bern, and Vorovsky cabled an appeal to him, "Please fulfill your promise immediately." Moor apparently responded with money, and at the beginning of December 1917 he returned to Stockholm. In the middle of January he traveled on to Petrograd, where he took part in the socialist conference held at the beginning of February. According to the Swiss legation, he also intervened with Soviet officials a number of times on behalf of Swiss citizens still in Russia.[16] In April he went to Berlin in Joffe's company, and there he played a role in Berzin's acceptance by the Swiss authorities.

When Moor finally returned to Switzerland in June, he immediately became a regular visitor at the Soviet mission—ironically, so was Grimm—but he also resumed his contacts with Romberg. The reports of Romberg and his agents suggest that Moor now did

more to represent Bolshevik interests to the Germans
than he did to press for German interests. In particular,
Moor carried to Romberg a complaint about the difficulties in organizing the courier service, and he also
made an effort to convince the Germans that the Bolsheviks had had nothing to do with the assassination of
the German ambassador in Russia, Count Mirbach, on
July 6.[17]

Moor also attempted to serve as a go-between for
Berzin with Swiss officials. Possibly he entertained visions of being named Swiss minister to Russia—Odier
had announced his retirement a year earlier but had
continued to serve on a temporary basis. In his capacity
as an elected official of the canton of Bern, Moor had
ready access into all governmental offices, and he could
even visit Willi Münzenberg at his place of internment
on the Lake of Zurich. In his memoirs, Münzenberg,
reflecting Moor's later fame as a Bolshevik, wrote warm-
ly of this occasion: "Among my many visitors was also
the dear old comrade Carl Moor, at present perhaps the
most interesting personality in the European labor
movement, whose friend I became later on." At the
time, however, Münzenberg could only wonder about
Moor's conversion to Bolshevism; epitomizing the confusion of all those who could not understand Moor's
activities, Münzenberg wrote to a friend, "I am moreover amazed how Moor today passes for a confidant of
the Bolsheviks."[18]

From July 27 to August 5, Moor was again in
Berlin, conferring with Joffe, and upon his return to
Bern he immediately visited the Federal Minister of
Economics, Bundesrat Edouard Schulthess, to whom he
explained that he was about to depart for Moscow.
Insisting that he had good relations with all circles in the
Russian capital, Moor let Schulthess know that he
would welcome a formal mission to represent Swiss

economic interests in Russia; in particular he was ready to discuss the matter of a new trade pact. Schulthess apparently raised no objection to Moor's engaging in such talks.

A few days after this interview, the Swiss press began to carry reports that Moor would possibly be named a special envoy to Russia. Reportedly Schulthess had charged Moor with the task of concluding a new trade agreement and a new pact on the treatment of each other's nationals, as well as arranging the formal recognition of the Soviet government by the Swiss. Schulthess's office immediately issued a denial, claiming that his interview with Moor had concerned "exclusively economic questions and in no way political affairs." [19] The Soviet mission also issued a declaration that Moor was acting on his own responsibility and initiative.

The entire affair was probably more the result of Moor's personal ambition than of any real political developments. Nevertheless, it made a major impact on the atmosphere in Switzerland. The ever-vigilant French military attaché distinguished two major lines of Bolshevik activity in Switzerland: one through a press bureau and the second Moor himself, although "the exact aim of this second means is mysteriously obscure." Moor, according to the French, was a pronounced Germanophile who had suddenly become rich in 1918, presumably with German money. Schulthess, who was accused of conducting a personal pro-German policy, probably had in fact given Moor no specific mission: "He has simply committed the mistake of being ignorant of the inordinate vanity and the senile loquacity of his compromising interlocutor." Moor, however, represented the idea of a Soviet-German alliance, the report concluded, and he was undoubtedly traveling to Russia with this object in mind. [20]

Moor left Bern in the company of Bratman, thereby offering another indication that in fact he was concerned with commercial matters, and, by chance, Swiss diplomats in Moscow asked him to intervene with the Soviet authorities on the question of the commercial treaty. Beyond the political furor which this caused in Bern, however, nothing came of his mission. In the fall, a Soviet diplomat, V. I. Miliutin, arrived in Bern with the task of negotiating a commercial treaty, but again circumstances also brought this effort to naught.

The controversy surrounding the Moor affair intensified at the end of August when news reached Bern of a speech which the self-appointed envoy had delivered before a trade union group in Moscow on August 22. He had come to Russia, he declared, to study what he could do on behalf of socialism in Switzerland. He gave thanks to Russian political emigrés in Switzerland for their work in educating the Swiss in "scientific socialism," and he heaped scorn on the Russian socialists who opposed Bolshevik rule. The proletariat of the West, he promised, would yet come to the help of the Russians.

Both French and British diplomats filed protests with the Swiss Foreign Office against the antiwestern tone of Moor's remarks. Although he was not a member of the Swiss government, they noted, he had traveled to Russia in agreement with a "prominent member of the Federal Council." In response Paravicini simply denied any responsibility for Moor's statements.[21]

Possibly in anticipation of embarrassment because of Moor's activities, the Swiss government had already named a new envoy to Russia, Albert Junod, Director of the Schweizerische Verkehrszentrale, who also held the title of Professor of National Economics and Economic Geography at the University of Neuchâtel. Government sources insisted that Junod was the ideal candidate for the post: he spoke six languages, including Russian, he had lived a while in Russia, and he had also served as

president of the Schweizerische Gesellschaft für kauf-
männisches Bildungswesen. The post obviously demanded such a man who could understand both Russian
and Swiss business interests.[22]

The socialist press greeted the appointment with
scorn. *La Sentinelle* of August 19 summed up the views
of the left by claiming that the Bundesrat had given
"proof of a complete lack of a sense of realities." The
government should have named a man of the left; Junod
could exert no influence in the new Russia: "Junod is a
theoretician and not a practitioner."

The French military attaché added his own criticism of the appointment as he reported that Swiss
political circles were surprised by the Bundesrat's decision. Swiss diplomats, he noted, were complaining that
the government was reaching outside the professional
service for its major appointments.[23] The Germans, on
the other hand, objected to Junod's French-Swiss background; Schulthess, however, assured them that the new
envoy was first of all a businessman who would be
concerned strictly with Swiss economic interests in
Russia. Schulthess would himself advise Junod against
becoming too involved in politics.[24]

Upon entering his new duties, Junod announced
that he would hold meetings throughout Switzerland
with persons concerned with the situation in Russia; in
one city after another his calendar was oversubscribed.
At the same time a Schweizerische Hilfs- und Kredit-
orengenossenschaft für Russland came into being, aimed
at protecting Swiss interests in Russia and at organizing
mutual assistance for persons hurt by the developments
in Russia. Junod dealt at length with representatives of
this group, but, as his critics hastened to point out, he
left Switzerland in the middle of October without having made a stop at the Soviet mission in Bern. (By way
of contrast, the English had carefully cleared the Lock-

hart mission to Russia with Maxim Litvinov.) He arrived in Moscow just in time to participate in the rupture between Switzerland and Russia.

By late summer, the situation in Russia was becoming ever more difficult. Most Entente diplomats left the country in July, leaving only unofficial agents such as Lockhart still in contact with Soviet authorities. Tensions grew apace, culminating in a crisis surrounding an unsuccessful attempt against Lenin's life on August 31, 1918. In a major crackdown on hostile elements within Russia, the Bolshevik regime, operating through the Cheka headed by Felix Dzerzhinsky, embarked on a "Red Terror," which included attacks on foreign missions and the arrest of Bruce Lockhart on the charge of having plotted to overthrow the Soviet government. Lockhart was eventually deported in exchange for a British agreement to allow Litvinov to return home.

The Swiss found their situation ever more difficult. Acting on behalf of the neutral missions in Russia and at the urging of the United States, Odier, on September 5, filed a protest with the Soviet government against its failure to observe the niceties of diplomatic immunity in its moves against what was left of the foreign missions. In the conclusion of his note, Odier declared that the neutral governments maintain the right yet to make claims for satisfaction from the Bolsheviks.

Chicherin answered the note with a sarcastic statement on September 12, declaring that the neutrals' action constituted an act of "gross interference" into Russia's internal affairs and was of itself unworthy of answer. Since, however, the Soviet government desired to publicize its activities and to explain them to the workers of the world, he would nevertheless respond.

The neutrals, Chicherin began, had chosen to complain of the treatment meted out to the bourgeoisie not by individuals but by the regime, "the Workers' and

Peasants' Government in its struggle with the class of exploiters." The Bolsheviks in answer would like to pose their own questions: Were the neutrals aware of the human losses caused by the four years of war? Were they aware of the bombings, the hunger? The bourgeoisie in the capitalist countries were conducting a White Terror against their own working classes: "The so-called neutral powers have not dared to protest with even one word against the White Terror or capital, yet they have not wanted to protest since the bourgeoisie of all neutral powers has aided the capital of the warring countries to continue the war, acquiring billions for provisions to both warring imperialist camps."

Furthermore, Chicherin continued, had the neutrals not heard anything about the bloody events in Ireland, the terror in Finland or in the Ukraine? Certainly they must have, but it never occurred to them to utter a word in protest: "The workers of Switzerland, Holland and Denmark have not yet arisen, but the governments of these countries are mobilizing armed force against them at the smallest protest of the popular masses."

The protests of the neutrals, he concluded, could have no effect on the policies of the Soviet government: "And we are sure that the popular masses of all countries, oppressed and terrorized by small groups of exploiters, will understand that in Russia force is used only in the name of the holy interests of the liberation of the popular masses, that they will not only understand us, but they will follow our path."[25]

In all the Swiss intervention won nothing from the Soviet government, but at the same time it gained the plaudits of the Entente. The British minister in Bern praised Odier's note for being "as vigorous as it was courageous." To Rumbold's surprise, Calonder, usually "very temperate in language," spoke "with great bitter-

ness and even with violence of the Bolshevik regime,"
complaining that the Swiss government was obliged to
maintain relations with the Bolsheviks only to protect
the Swiss still in Russia.[26]

Pro-Soviet sources in Switzerland reprinted the exchange between Odier and Chicherin for mass distribution in Switzerland, claiming victory for the cause of
social revolution. This eventually gave rise to the charge,
often repeated by Entente intelligence sources, that a
revolutionary call to arms signed by Chicherin was being
circulated in Swiss radical circles.[27]

At the end of September, Fritz Platten and thirteen other Social Democratic deputies in the Swiss national council, The Nationalrat, filed an interpellation
demanding to know why the Swiss government had not
yet gained de jure recognition to the Soviet mission. The
government replied simply that in view of the uncertain
situation in Russia, such recognition was impossible.

In all, the Berzin mission could do little on problems of Soviet-Swiss relations; indeed, such activity was
apparently only a secondary function of the mission.
The Swiss might refuse to withdraw their diplomats as
the Entente did, but neither would Bern embark on any
major initiatives of its own. The Swiss deliberately pat-
terned their official attitudes toward the Bolsheviks
after the models offered by the Great Powers. For the
Bolsheviks, the Swiss government represented more a
necessary evil to deal with than an enticing partner.

6: PERSONALITIES AND ASSIGNMENTS

When the Soviet mission opened for business on the Schwanengasse, Paravicini established a watch on the building. His agents had seen no suspicious activity previously at Shklovsky's home, and now they observed little untoward activity in the new quarters. To be sure, there was a considerable traffic of visitors, especially Russian soldiers, but this was to be expected. Of perhaps greater significance, the watch noted that Platten visited the mission five or six times in the first month of its operation, Moor came twice, and Grimm two or three times. (The English referred to Platten, Grimm and Moor, together with Ernst Nobs, as the "Swiss counterpart" of the Bolshevik "machinery in Switzerland.")[1]

Bern abounded with stories about the mission. Generally, Berzin, who had already impressed Mercier favorably, came off well in the diplomatic gossip; the Austrian minister characterized him as a "blond, slender blue-eyed, highly good-natured and enthusiastic appearing young man, tubercular, and in contrast to his better known colleagues a Christian, a Latvian born in Riga."[2] Berzin's colleagues did not come off so well. Shklovsky, Paravicini's deputy declared, was a "small, clever Jew with a pointed beard, about 45 years old, who originally came in dressed in very primitive Bolshevik fashion, visibly became more elegant, and eventually left Bern again in exactly his original suit."[3] In discussing the rest of the mission, the diplomats seemed to vie in repeating derogatory stories; the British minister reported that a hotel director had asked his Bolshevik guests to eat in their rooms "in order not to rob the other guests of appetite for those viands which the rationing system still permits of retention on the dwindling menus."[4]

Berzin spent little time in Bern. The watch observed him at the mission on June 24, but the next day, after meeting with Calonder, he left the city for Sigriswyl on the Beatenberg, where he rented rooms in the pension Alpenruhe. He returned again for the day on June 29. According to many who knew him, Berzin's health at this time was poor. Lenin's letters demonstrated great concern for Berzin's health: "And so, stay well and strictly observe your regimen." On October 15 he wrote, "Convalesce seriously and do not leave the sanatorium. Communicate by telephone, but send a deputy to meetings." Three days later he added, "If the doctors said to stay in bed, then not a step out of the sanatorium. . . . You can easily refuse receptions, spend ¼ hour on reports on 'affairs' and conversations about 'affairs,' one and ¾ hours on directing everything else. Choose *responsible persons.*" On November 1, Lenin advised, "Lie and strictly recover; you must not stay in Bern but in the mountains in the sun where there are a telephone and a railroad, and you can send a secretary and they can come to you."[5]

According to the local postmaster in Sigriswyl, Berzin received little mail, but the official speculated that he seemed to be receiving most of the revolutionary newspapers of the world. Berzin also spent a great deal of time on the telephone, conferring with Liubov Pokrovskaia of the mission; to the frustration of the Swiss, they spoke only in Russian.

In Berzin's absence, Grigorii Shklovsky handled the day-to-day administration of the mission. A long-time resident of Bern, he received a doctorate in chemistry from the university in 1917 and then returned to Russia.[6] After the Bolshevik revolution he held a post in the Moscow city administration, but when the Berzin mission was being assembled, he accepted the opportunity to return to Bern, where he had left his family.

Shklovsky held the title of Counsellor, received visitors in Berzin's absence, dealt with the Swiss Foreign Office, and handled the finances of the mission. To many observers, he appeared to be the mastermind of Bolshevik activities in Switzerland; in fact, he was just the administrator and treasurer.

The mission's financial affairs were the focus of the most speculation by outsiders. Rumors of the amount at its disposal ranged up to fifty million francs. Gossip spoke of enormous deposits in banks in Basel, Zurich, and Geneva; contrary stories argued that the bulk of the Russian money did not lie in the banks but rather in the pockets and safety deposit boxes of local radicals. Taking note of these stories, the Swiss government gave some consideration to the idea of possibly seizing this Bolshevik money—if it could find it—in payment of Swiss claims against the Soviet government.[7]

Shklovsky's own personal account at the Schweizerische Volksbank in Bern recorded total deposits of 931,211.65 francs in the period from June 20 to October 31, 1918. This by no means included all the money which passed through his hands, as Swiss bank officials had records of over a million rubles changed by Shklovsky and Boris Lifschitz in the period between July 31 and August 12, while only 331,500 Swiss francs were added to Shklovsky's bank account in this period. (On August 13, Shklovsky offered another 200,000 rubles for sale but then withdrew them because of an unfavorable rate of exchange.) On September 5, Lifschitz changed another million rubles in "Duma notes," but only 100,000 francs were deposited on September 6. In all, Swiss officials found records for the exchange of about 2.5 million rubles—something over 3 million francs at that time.[8]

Shklovsky's bank records did not make clear the

recipients of all the money paid out, but they established payments of 201,410 francs to Maxim Rivosh, presumably for distribution among Russian students in Switzerland; 52,000 to Stefan Bratman, probably for Russian soldiers; 58,205 to Sergei Petropavlovsky, for the Soviet press agency in Bern; and 139,250 to Peters Starke, for unknown purposes. The figures of themselves reveal nothing startling, but they point rather definitely to several areas of activity by the Soviet mission.[9]

The structure of the mission did not lend itself to simple diagramming since the members themselves apparently had no firm conception of hierarchical organization. The assignment of traditional diplomatic posts such as counsellor, secretary, courier, and consul had little meaning. Zalkind, Pokrovskaia and Nikolai Liubarsky offer cases in point.

On June 18 the mission informed the Swiss Political Department that Zalkind had been named Russian Consul General for Switzerland; the document named no site for his activity. Since consulates did not fall under normal diplomatic protocol, the Russians still did not present Zalkind's credentials to the government. Zalkind remained in Switzerland without the "blue card" which signified diplomatic status; so far as the Swiss government was concerned, he was a private Soviet citizen, however well publicized and observed.

In practice Zalkind seems to have directed the overall propaganda activity of the Bolsheviks in Switzerland as well as coordinating the mission's work among the emigrés. He was at least Shklovsky's equal as far as prestige and authority in the mission were concerned.[10] Although Colonel Pageot repeatedly insisted that Zalkind had established and was maintaining a Bolshevik office in Zurich, Zurich officials tended to deny this. Zalkind's mailing address was an office in the Bolshevik mission in Bern, but he traveled a great deal, dealing with Platten and Rivosh in Zurich, Guilbeaux in Geneva, and others.

Pokrovskaia, the wife of the noted historian M. N. Pokrovsky, was nominally a secretary of the mission. On May 16, upon reporting Pokrovskaia's appointment, Odier had warned that she had been charged "with provoking, through Bolshevik propaganda, troubles among the Swiss workers." In Switzerland she was responsible for choosing Russian publications for translation and distribution as well as for the selection of information for transmittal to either the I.S.C. in Stockholm or to the Soviet government. Berzin's frequent telephone calls probably testified to her importance; she may well have been a channel of communications between Berzin and Zalkind since she, alone among the members of the mission, was staying in the same hotel as Zalkind.

Nikolai Markovich Liubarsky, in addition to his role as First Secretary of the mission, was an Italian specialist, handling relations with Italians in Switzerland as well as directing the sending of materials into Italy. He had lived in Capri before the war, and when he served in the Russian army, his wife had remained in Italy. In 1918, after dealing with many obstacles and formalities posed by Italian authorities, his wife came to Switzerland to join him. With Zalkind, Liubarsky was an observer at the Swiss workers' conference held in Basel at the end of July.

The mission recruited a large part of its office staff from among the Russian emigrés already in Switzerland, but it also demonstrated the internationalist outlook of the Soviet government by hiring a number of non-Russians, including the Dutch radical Herman Gorter, [11] several Swiss, an Austrian, and a Serb. Even among its personnel who were former subjects of the Tsarist Empire, the mission presented a radically different appearance from that of former Russian missions, which had been dominated by Great Russians or possibly Russified Baltic Germans. In Berzin's mission the preponderance seemed to be Jewish and Latvian.

Among the better known emigrés who came to work for the mission was Sofia Dzerzhinskaia, the wife of Felix Dzerzhinsky. Separated from her husband since before the war, she had lived in Switzerland with the Bratman family, and in September 1918 she followed the lead of her friends in taking work with the mission. She later claimed to Swiss authorities that she had simply sorted mail, but in fact she seems to have been Shklovsky's secretary.

Because of Dzerzhinskaia's presence, the mission briefly hosted Dzerzhinsky himself. Exhausted by his work during the Red Terror of the month of September, Dzerzhinsky was ordered to take a vacation; in the guise of a diplomatic courier, Feliks Damanski, he came to Switzerland to visit his wife. (Accompanying him was Varlaam Avanesov, another Cheka official.) As all touring fathers do in Bern, Dzerzhinsky immediately took his son to feed the bears, but the Dzerzhinskys soon decided to spend a week outside of the city, somewhere where Dzerzhinsky could relax. After a brief visit to Lucerne, the three made their way to Lugano, where Dzerzhinsky had an unexpected shock.

Sitting in a small boat on the Lake of Lugano, Dzerzhinsky suddenly came face to face with Bruce Lockhart, who was on the deck of a passing excursion boat: "Feliks recognized him immediately. . . . The English spy, however, fortunately did not recognize Feliks; his appearance had so changed. Besides, this enemy could not have imagined that the chairman of the Cheka was in Switzerland."

To be sure, Dzerzhinsky proved eminently successful in maintaining his anonymity in Switzerland. The

Swiss became aware of his visit only after his wife's memoirs had been published in 1964.[12] A British agent in Lugano noted the presence of a Russian courier named "Drwanski," who had contacts with local "revolutionary" elements, but he too indicated no awareness of the true identity of the man. On the other hand, Dzerzhinskaia may have been guilty of a certain overdramatization in her account. In his memoirs, Lockhart only once mentioned seeing Dzerzhinsky; during his imprisonment in September he was questioned mainly by a Latvian Chekist named Peters, who had once lived in London. Dzerzhinsky's anonymity may not have been in such danger as his wife indicated. Dzerzhinsky left Switzerland on October 23.[13]

Interned Russian soldiers including both escaped prisoners of war coming from Austria and Germany and also deserters from the Russian forces in France, occupied the time of a number of the mission's employees, whom the mission in fact shared with the Russian Red Cross. Holzmann had already dealt directly with the internees. In 1914 a Russian revolutionary emigré had proclaimed that the Russian soldiers taken prisoner by the Central Powers "were our army"; the Bolsheviks seemed to share this view in 1918.

The Swiss welcomed all efforts to help the internees materially, but at times they felt that the Bolsheviks stirred up more trouble than they resolved. On June 13, for example, a member of the mission, Ernst Bolin, appeared in Reinach to harangue the Russian soldiers there, insisting that they were being treated like slaves. He had come, he declared, to help them by buying them clothes, boots, and other necessities. The local Swiss were most impressed by the money he wielded; on the fourteenth, when he placed a telephone call to the mission in Bern, he attempted to pay with a 1000 franc note.

At the beginning of August, Sergei Bagotsky arrived

as the head of the Commission of the Russian Red Cross in Switzerland, charged with helping the soldiers. At the time he received his visa in Moscow, the Swiss consul warned that Bagotsky probably had "Bolshevik propaganda as his principal mission in Switzerland,"[14] but Bagotsky, a medical doctor, had extensive experience in both revolutionary activities and refugee relief. For many years he had directed the Cracow Union for Aid to Political Prisoners and Exiles; in 1914 he had moved this organization from Austria to Switzerland, where it became a part of the Liga schweizerischer Hilfsvereine für russische Gefangene und Verbannte. In 1917 he had served as the secretary of the Central Committee for the Repatriation of Russian Emigrés, and he had returned to Russia in January 1918. He had also on occasion served as a personal physician to Lenin and his wife.

Upon his arrival in Switzerland in August, Bagotsky immediately succeeded in unseating the representatives of the old regime, who had still been representing Russia in the International Red Cross organization. (Bagotsky's group was known as the "Third Russian Red Cross" mission.) In Bagotsky's wake came another emissary from Russia, R. A. Lamm, representing the Moscow Committee for Aid to War Prisoners, who also settled in Bern. Together the two quickly won the recognition of the Swiss government, and over the protests of the anti-Bolshevik Russians, they monopolized the handling of the interned Russian soldiers.

The Swiss seemed particularly relieved at the eagerness of the Bolshevik emissaries to take over the care of the Russian deserters from France, who had obviously had nothing to do with the previous Russian diplomatic missions. As a result of negotiations between the Political Department and the Soviet mission, the Swiss recognized Bagotsky's Red Cross mission as independent of the diplomatic mission, as an autonomous agency, although the two shared many employees.

As his assistant, Bagotsky chose Ilia Shneerson, a Russian emigré who had lived in Switzerland since 1914. Shneerson, who spoke German poorly, had failed in his attempt to obtain work from Shklovsky in May, but in September he began to work part-time as assistant to Stefan Bratman in the mission and part-time with Bagotsky. After three weeks, Shneerson became Bagotsky's full-time assistant.

A less fortunate choice as an employee was Vladimir Rembelinsky, a veteran Bolshevik, who served briefly as the Red Cross's representative in Lausanne. Rembelinsky had lived in Lausanne since before the war, but in 1918 he made a brief trip to Russia. Upon his return to Lausanne in the fall of 1918, he began to work for Bagotsky, but almost immediately he ran afoul of an interview which he gave to Charles Naine's newspaper *Le Droit du peuple*. Naine interpreted his statements as indicating that he was opposed to the use of violence in carrying out social revolution. Rembelinsky wrote an angry letter to Naine protesting that he had meant no such thing, but the damage was done. Endorsement of the use of violence was a key issue at this time in distinguishing supporters of the Bolshevik revolution from pacifists, and Rembelinsky was released from his job with the Red Cross.[15]

According to Bagotsky's own testimony, the Soviet government sent one million rubles by diplomatic courier to Bern to launch the work of his commission, but the mission gave him only 565,000 Swiss francs, which he then deposited in a bank in Bern.[16] The mission turned over to him the care of all the military internees, but Bagotsky also undertook to help the various pro-Bolshevik emigré aid groups in Basel, Zurich, and Geneva.

Bagotsky directed his main effort toward the military internees. It had been the practice of the Swiss government to send all the escaped Russians, whether from France or Germany, to Fribourg, on the border between the German and French-speaking parts of Switzerland. Once a group of some thirty to forty had been collected they would be taken to Bern where at one time Onu's legation, subsequently Berzin's mission, and now Bagotsky's office would usually provide them with clothing and basic necessities. Then the Swiss would take them to work camps where they lived under military style discipline and engaged in agricultural work.

The Swiss treated the escaped prisoners and deserters in the same fashion, although from the Russian point of view, the two groups represented different legal problems. Onu had had nothing to do with the deserters, but Berzin and Bagotsky were able to arrange the return of over nine hundred of them in two train loads through Germany in the summer and fall of 1918.[17] On the other hand, the escaped prisoners, who numbered about three hundred, could not travel through the territory of the Central Powers, and while their legal status in Switzerland was clear, they required continued care.

Bagotsky immediately sought to improve the conditions in which the soldiers lived, and he protested the practice of treating the Russian deserters in the same manner as the Swiss treated German and French deserters. Russia, he argued, had now left the war. Although he made little headway in this regard, he did succeed in providing some special treatment for the Russians.

After his first inspection trips, Bagotsky complained that the Russians had to live in poorly kept barracks, unheated at night and exposed to the elements. The food was generally bad and the pay for their work—seventy to eighty-five centimes per hour—inadequate. (Holzmann, upon his return to Russia in July, insisted that the conditions were so bad that Russian soldiers even chose to flee back to confinement in Austria; the Swiss disputed these assertions.)

At Bagotsky's insistence, the Swiss agreed that after being assembled at Fribourg, the fugitives could relax for two weeks at a pension which Bagotsky had rented at Interlaken. (Bagotsky's enemies claimed that the pension, as well as quarters which Bagotsky had rented for soldiers in Bern, amounted to a Bolshevik training camp; they frequently named Zalkind as the director.) In addition, ill internees could go to either of the two sanatoria which the Russian Red Cross established, one in Clarens for convalescents and one in Davos for those suffering from tuberculosis. Also, those ex-prisoners with special talents and abilities were to be offered a chance to find appropriate jobs.[18]

After the expulsion of the Soviet mission in November, the Red Cross commission undertook the support of all needy Russians in Switzerland, and it also acted as an informal channel of communication between the Swiss and the Soviet governments in subsequent years. The Political Department itself paid Bagotsky a compliment when, in December 1918, in response to a complaint lodged by an American diplomat, it emphasized that Bagotsky and his wife had worked "intensively and in useful fashion" on behalf of the escaped prisoners. In all, Bagotsky was to remain in Switzerland until 1936.

Strangely enough, the diplomatic mission housed opposition elements too, as at least six Left Socialist Revolutionaries came to Switzerland under the cover of the diplomatic service. These included Isaac Steinberg, former People's Commissar of Justice, who served as a legal specialist, and two couriers, Alexander Shreider and Mark Natanson. Shreider had previously served as Steinberg's assistant, and Natanson was one of the senior leaders of the Socialist Revolutionary Party. All these men left Russia in the course of June 1918, and their departure was related to the break between their party and the Bolsheviks, epitomized by the assassination of the German ambassador to Soviet Russia, Count W. Mirbach, on July 6, 1918.

In November 1917, the Left Socialist Revolutionaries, splitting away from their Right colleagues, supported the new Bolshevik government in Russia and accepted the role of a junior partner in a coalition government. Steinberg became Commissar of Justice at that time. Like the left wing of the Bolshevik Party, however, the Socialist Revolutionaries had opposed signing the Treaty of Brest-Litovsk with Imperial Germany. This dissatisfaction with the Bolsheviks' foreign policy smoldered in subsequent months, fanned by growing differences over agrarian policies. At the end of June and the beginning of July, the Left Socialist Revolutionaries openly announced their opposition to Bolshevik policies, and two members of the party assassinated the German ambassador in a vain hope of forcing a renewal of hostilities between Germany and Russia.[19] The Bolshevik government proved able to survive the diplomatic crisis without being forced to go to war, but an attempt by another Socialist Revolutionary to assassinate Lenin on August 31 resulted in the Red Terror of September.

The Central Committee of the Left Socialist Revolutionaries made its decision to kill Mirbach on June 24; Steinberg and Natanson had already left the country. [20] Shreider now undertook the charge to join Steinberg in Switzerland and to propagandize the views of the party in Western Europe. On June 28 he resigned his post as Commissar of Justice for the region of Moscow, and the following day he left the country, carrying a diplomatic passport as a courier and taking 400,000 rubles in the event that a diplomatic rupture between Russia and Germany should cut off the sending of money later. (Shreider's sudden move did not go unnoticed, as the Swiss consul in Moscow noted a newspaper item announcing Shreider's resignation and departure.)[21]

The Soviet government, it might be noted, still had no professional diplomatic courier service—indeed, with the expectation of world revolution, such a service probably seemed unnecessary—and therefore the Commissariat of Foreign Affairs seemed ready to send as couriers almost anyone who came forward with reasonably acceptable credentials. In May and June Karl Radek had the responsibility of naming these couriers; ironically, Joffe, in defending Natanson's role as a courier, was unknowingly helping enemies of the Bolshevik regime. Once in Switzerland, Shreider and Steinberg proceeded about their business. Natanson, a sick man, apparently played no major role in their work, although he kept in close touch with them. (In September he underwent an operation for a respiratory disorder, and he died the next year.) Shreider and Steinberg both opened accounts at the Eidgenössische Bank in Bern, depositing 50,000 francs each on July 12. In one safety deposit box at the Banque Federale in Lausanne, they stored 104,500 rubles and 10,000 francs, in another, 30 to 35,000 francs. They were also probably the source of the 60,000 francs which Joseph Chapiro, a Socialist Revolutionary living in Geneva, later admitted receiving from an unidentified person in the Soviet mission. Steinberg held a post as legal advisor in the Soviet mission, but Shreider maintained no connection with it.

Most western observers seemed to misunderstand their purpose. Their frequent meetings with socialists of other countries, watched and reported by various political agents, were interpreted as attempting to propagandize the Bolshevik cause. In fact, while they were, to be sure, advocating social revolution, they were also attempting to explain the policies of the Left Socialist Revolutionaries. Western observers, for instance, drew the worst conclusions from a visit made to Zurich on July 13 by Natanson, at which time he spoke with Platten and other Swiss Socialists. Yet on July 17,

Volksrecht published a long interview with an unnamed Left Socialist Revolutionary, undoubtedly Natanson, explaining the reasons of the Left SR's in going into the opposition. Nonsocialists could not seem to comprehend the dynamics of Soviet politics.

Shreider later claimed that his group had published two books and two pamphlets in Switzerland: Boris Kamkov *Les socialistes révolutionnaires de gauche* (Kamkov, once an emigré in Switzerland, was one of the leaders of the opposition in Russia); Steinberg, *Pourquoi nous sommes contre la paix de Brest-Litowsk;* Steinberg and Shreider, *La Russie socialiste;* and Shreider, *L'organisation judiciare de la Russie des Soviets.* In addition, the two men sought to establish contacts with socialist intellectuals in French-speaking Switzerland, and Shreider may well have contributed to many of Paul Graber's attacks on the Bolshevik Red Terror, published in the columns of *La Sentinelle* in September and October. "The Bolsheviks have compromised the success of world socialism," Graber wrote: "We regret this mistake."[22]

In September Shreider considered his work in Switzerland done and sought to return home, but he found the way closed. Neither France nor the Central Powers would consider giving him a visa, and Berzin would have nothing to do with him. "Is it possible that Soviet Russia will not allow us revolutionary socialists to return?" he wrote in anguish to Natanson on September 23. "I just cannot imagine how to return to Russia." For the time being he had to linger on in Switzerland. [23]

Nor were the Socialist Revolutionaries the only opposition elements. Two minor employees of the mission, who were known to spend a great many evenings in "Tingel-Tangel Wirtschaften," music halls, established close contact with local Latvians, including Wladimir Ellansky (Klavin), a correspondent of the conservative

Bern newspaper *Der Bund.* (Ellansky and Abram Charasch of the *Neue Zürcher Zeitung* were probably the
two most knowledgeable commentators writing about
Russia in the nonsocialist Swiss press.) But while *Der
Bund* often served as an outlet for governmental pronouncements, the officials in the police department and
the foreign office seemed to grasp little of Ellansky's
knowledgeable articles.[24]

In another example of western incomprehension of
the nature and character of the Bolshevik mission, Sir
Horace Rumbold at one time singled out Adam Kahan,
who had come as a diplomatic courier, as the "leading
spirit" of the mission. Since Kahan had once worked as
a waiter in Vienna, Bern, and Petrograd before assuming
his brief diplomatic career, he offered a particularly
vulnerable target for sarcastic attacks on the mission. In
fact, Kahan was an unhappy individual who kept a
notebook at home in which he drafted letters to Lenin
and to the Soviet government complaining about the
mission, charging Shklovsky with mishandling funds and
Zalkind with gambling.[25]

The mission indeed had its full share of internal
antagonisms even without Kahan's strange behavior.
Berzin apparently complained to Moscow about some of
his colleagues, and Lenin wrote to him in a reassuring
tone. In a letter of October 18, Lenin spoke of "fools"
and "idiots" in the mission and complained that Berzin
seemed to have no responsible people in his mission,
with the exception of his secretary Maurice Leiteisen.
On November 1, Lenin declared, "I hear that everyone
has been quarreling at your place. We will recall Shklovsky and Zalkind. If you write anything, I will sign your
orders (to your subordinates) so that they cannot quar-
rel and will strictly fulfill your orders."[26]

The nature of Berzin's disagreement with Zalkind
and Shklovsky remains unclear. Lenin had had some

troubles with Shklovsky in the winter of 1916-1917, [27] and perhaps this had recurred. Zalkind may have been acting too independently for Berzin's taste. The dispute which arose between Guilbeaux and Balabanova also probably played a role here. Zalkind was an enthusiastic supporter of Guilbeaux, while Berzin apparently harbored some reservations about him. In any case, Lenin's readiness to recall both Shklovsky and Zalkind offers a key for understanding the different responses which Berzin and Shklovsky gave to Swiss officials at the beginning of November when the question arose of Zalkind's expulsion from Switzerland.

7: INFORMATION AND PROPAGANDA

When Berzin accepted his assignment as envoy to Switzerland, Lenin made clear to him that his task lay not in "purely diplomatic work," since "there was not much that could be accomplished in this direction," but rather that Switzerland was the ideal point from which to inform the West about events in Russia. "All his advice," Berzin later recounted, "chiefly concerned this aspect of our work. In connection with this he never stopped repeating: 'It is necessary to work in such a way that you can never be accused of propaganda. There is a sort of freedom and democracy in Switzerland; there we always found shelter as emigrés and freely published our organs. There can be no legal obstacles for an interview in the newspapers, for articles, for publishing brochures about Russia, etc.' "[1]

In his personal letters to Berzin, Lenin always emphasized the problems of propaganda and information. Berzin later characterized these concerns as the major work of his mission, and in a negative fashion he gave emphasis to this by censoring those sections out of Lenin's letters when he published them in 1925 on the anniversary of Lenin's death. The omitted passages, as restored in the fifth edition of Lenin's writings published by the Institute of Marxism-Leninism, almost all concerned the propaganda activities of the mission, particularly the publication of Lenin's own polemical writing. Berzin explained his ellipses by saying that it was not yet time, in 1925, to discuss his work in Switzerland.

In a letter of August 3, delivered by returning

Italian prisoners of war, Lenin recommended that Berzin aid them in publishing and distributing works written in Italian. He also exclaimed, "For God's sake, don't spare money on publication (in German, French, Italian, English languages), and faster, faster." On October 15, he complained that Berzin had sent publications only to Ia. M. Sverdlov, the head of the Soviet government: "It would not be a sin to send me this collection too." In addition he considered the volume of publication too small: "Little! Little!! Little!!! Take a group of translators and publish 10 times as much. [Edmondo] Peluso can (and should) write three brochures a week (on all themes, compilations from our newspapers—you give the *themes* and a list of articles for compilation). His article in *Droit du Peuple* ("Counterrevolutionaries") is good. Pay him well and publish ten times as much. (Hire translators for publications in four languages: French, German, English, and Italian. You have nothing in the last two. Scandal! Scandal!!) You have *much* money. (Without fail send a note on the sums expended by you.) We will give *more and more, without accounting.* Write how much. It is necessary to publish 100 times as much, in four languages, booklets of 4, 8, 16, and 32 pages. *Hire* people for this."[2]

Lenin was also concerned with the publication of his own work: "When will my *State and Revolution* appear? Send it to me immediately. For the French translation (by no means holding it up) I would add something on Vandervelde. Write or telegraph." On October 25 he questioned, "When will the French edition of *State and Revolution* appear? Will I have time to write an introduction against Vandervelde?" When Lenin received the German translation of *State and Revolution* he complained that the epilogue had not been dated: "And the *whole* purpose is to show that the *epilogue* was written *after* the October Revolution.

Namely November 30, 1917. Is it possible to add a slip on this?"[3]

When *Pravda* of September 20 carried excerpts from an article by the German Socialist Karl Kautsky attacking Bolshevism, Lenin immediately protested to Berzin: "The disgraceful rubbish, the childish babble, and the very banal opportunism of Kautsky arouse the question: why are we doing nothing for the struggle with Kautsky's *theoretical* debasement of Marxism? . . . Kautsky has found nothing better than to write now against the Bolsheviks." In response the Bolsheviks should encourage German radicals to criticize Kautsky; they should hurry with the publication of *State and Revolution*. Lenin requested that Berzin provide him with the full text of Kautsky's article, as well as any other writings of his about the Bolsheviks.[4]

On October 11, *Pravda* carried an article by Lenin entitled "The Proletarian Revolution and the Renegade Kautsky." Lenin immediately ordered the Commissariat of Foreign Affairs to send copies to the Soviet diplomatic representatives abroad, and at the same time he worked feverishly to complete a sizeable brochure under the same title. On November 1, he sent off one-half of the manuscript to Berzin with orders that it be translated into German, French, and Italian as soon as possible.[5]

In order to carry out the tasks of publication and propaganda, the Soviet mission in Bern chose to establish an autonomous agency, nominally independent of the mission, and called "Russische Nachrichten" (Russian News). This was done at the end of May, and the direction of the enterprise was given to Nikolai Zamiatin. A student about forty years old, Zamiatin had been active for some time in the small Bolshevik circle in Lausanne, which produced a number of important recruits for the Bolsheviks. Holzmann had apparently come with orders to seek Zamiatin out, for in a telegram to Vorovsky on February 23, he reported having seen both Platten and Zamiatin. When Zalkind arrived in Zurich, Zamiatin moved there, and he accompanied Holzmann and Zalkind to Bern on May 21 when they joined the Soviet mission. He may have returned to Zurich on May 24, but by the end of the month he was again in Bern at the head of Russische Nachrichten.

In June Zamiatin hired as his assistant James Reich, an Austrian citizen, whom he had met in Zurich, and Reich, who occasionally published under the name James Gordon, eventually came to direct the agency as Zamiatin first took the task of organizing an information office within the mission and finally, in September, departed for Russia. (Reich continued to correspond with him in Moscow.)

Reich, born in Lvov in 1886, had studied in Bern and Zurich from 1906 to 1912. In 1914-1915 he served in the Austrian army but was released because of problems with his heart. He returned to Zurich in 1915, actively participated in radical activities, but was unemployed when Zamiatin offered him work. Nominally the director of Russische Nachrichten, Reich was in fact probably more a figurehead, dependent on Zalkind and Pokrovskaia.[6]

Sometime after his employment, Reich proposed a formal plan of organization for Russische Nachrichten, which, although it was never formally promulgated, defined the activity of the agency. Reich proposed three divisions: press service, publishing, and survey of the European press. In practice, the third division tended to merge with the first.

In his proposal, Reich identified Pokrovskaia, Jules Wetzosol, Zalkind, and himself as being concerned with the first division. Liubarsky, Zalkind, Zamiatin, and Sergei Petropavlovsky handled the problems of publishing, and Liubarsky, Zamiatin, and Petropavlovsky directed the survey of the European press. Petropavlovsky also served as treasurer of the organization.[7] Sergei Petropavlovsky, born in 1886, married with two children, had come to Lausanne as a student in 1915. In the summer of 1917 he had been forced to give up his studies when his parents could no longer send him money, and in the fall of that year he had moved to Bern. He had first worked for the "Second Red Cross mission," sent by the Provisional Government, but in June 1918 he lost this job. Zamiatin, whom he knew from Lausanne, then hired him at Russische Nachrichten. When questioned later by Swiss authorities, Petropavlovsky claimed that his job had consisted simply in reading newspapers, but in fact he handled the money which Shklovsky gave the agency for its work.[8]

According to Reich, the agency received all its information on Soviet Russia in Russian language materials provided by the mission and presumably carried by diplomatic courier. Pokrovskaia surveyed the material and decided which items were to be translated into German or French. Reich consistently argued that the agency was directly subordinated to the Soviet government and was independent of the mission, although he admitted that since he was "in active personal contact" with members of the mission, he was well oriented as to where Russische Nachrichten should put emphasis.

The agency's major public effort involved publication of a daily news bulletin—first appearing in hectographed, then mimeographed, and finally printed form, in both German, *Russische Nachrichten* (200 issues), and French, *Nouvelles de Russie* (160 issues). (The French and the German issues were separate publications, not just translations.) A typical run of *Russische Nachrichten*, at its peak, was 225-230 copies. In Reich's words, "There was no subscription to *Russische Nach-*

richten. They were sent free of charge to the press as well as to interested private persons." *Russische Nachrichten* gradually found greater acceptance by the bourgeois press; by the time of the attempt on Lenin's life at the end of August, the credit "rn" was appearing regularly even in *Der Bund* and *Die Neue Zürcher Zeitung.* The agency also began to publish another bulletin, *Sozialistische Korrespondenz,* aimed specifically at the socialist press in Switzerland. *Sozialistische Korrespondenz,* which appeared irregularly, came out under Fritz Platten's name. The policy of *Russische Nachrichten* aimed at publicizing the "positive accomplishments of the Soviet government especially in the cultural field." It even commissioned articles by Anatole Lunacharsky, "Education of the Proletariat," and by Krupskaya, "Life in Russian Schools."

In a report dated September 27, the staff of the agency claimed that its news releases were appearing "almost regularly" in the Swiss press, even receiving honoraria from the *Neue Zürcher Zeitung.* In addition, releases appeared in France "from time to time"; in Holland, where interest seemed very high; in Italy, through the pages of *Avanti;* and in the Scandinavian countries. The agency did not attempt to send its material to England "because of the special, well-organized censorship," but it was trying to place items there through "the correspondence of a third party," probably meaning the efforts of Edmondo Peluso, discussed below. The influence of *Russische Nachrichten* was growing, the report concluded, pointing to a growing volume of mail as well as to the press citations.[9]

The publication division of the agency had a particularly important job as it arranged the translation and publication of a number of major works by the leaders of the Soviet government. In order to disguise the role of *Russische Nachrichten,* Zamiatin and Reich turned to the Promachos Verlag, a small publishing house in Belp, near Bern, which in its less than three years of existence had already run into trouble with the Swiss police for putting out works advocating abortion. Reich first asked the house for an estimate on one work, Trotsky's account of the October Revolution. After an agreement had been made, he pressed the house to allow Russische Nachrichten to apply the name of the Promachos Verlag to books printed elsewhere. The management hesitated at first, but influenced by sympathy for the cause as well as by the amount of business involved, it finally agreed. As a result, most of the publications of the Promachos Verlag, in contract with Russische Nachrichten, were printed by the Genossenschaftsbuchdruckerei in Basel. Although the director of Promachos, Hans Jordi, demanded the right to review all manuscripts which would bear his firm's name, Russische Nachrichten declared that this would only complicate matters. Jordi yielded.

Eventually, the publisher came to learn of new books bearing its name when the printers reported that the finished copies would arrive on a certain day. Promachos, moreover, did not receive the entire run; Russische Nachrichten took several hundred copies for its own purposes. Russische Nachrichten took over all problems of advertising and distributing review copies. There was not enough time before the breakup of the operation in November 1918 for the two sides to regulate all the financial considerations of the enterprise. [10]

Most of the works published under the Promachos label were written by Lenin and Trotsky. Lenin's works included, *Die nächsten Aufgaben der Sowjet-Macht, Ein Brief an die amerikanischen Arbeiter, Der Kampf um das Brot, Die proletarische Revolution und der Renegat Kautsky, Staat und Revolution.* French editions included *Les Problèmes présents du pouvoir des soviets* (published by *Demain*) and *La Tâche des representants de la gauche de Zimmerwald dans le Parti Socialiste Suisse* (published by *La Nouvelle Internationale*). Trotsky's works included *Arbeit, Disziplin und Ordnung werden die sozialistische Sowjet-Republik retten, Von der Oktober Revolution bis zum Brester Friedensvertrag, Die Sowjet-Macht und der internationale Imperialismus,* and *De la Révolution d'Octobre à la paix de Brest-Litovsk* (published by *Demain*). Other publications which appeared under the direction of the Russische Nachrichten were: Viator (Karl Radek), *Die internationale Lage Russlands; L'Oeuvre économique de la Russie socialiste;* Morgan Philips Price, *The Truth about the Allied Intervention* (in French, German, and English); and Jacques Sadoul, *Notes sur la révolution bolchevique.*

The publication of Sadoul's account of the revolution presented an interesting example of the operation of Russische Nachrichten. A French socialist who had been assigned to his government's military mission in Russia in October 1917, Sadoul had become increasingly disenchanted with his own government's policies toward the Bolshevik regime and increasingly sympathetic to the efforts of Lenin and Trotsky to maintain control of the country. His letters to Albert Thomas had been allegedly seized by Soviet authorities during raids made on Entente missions in Russia, but in fact Sadoul had already prepared them for publication. The Soviet government sent the manuscript to the mission in Bern for printing.

Sadoul had prefaced his work with two open letters addressed to Romain Rolland. (Writing open letters to Rolland was a fashionable intellectual tactic at this time.) Deciding to capitalize on Rolland's name, Berzin and Zalkind asked Henri Guilbeaux to persuade Rolland to write an introduction to the published diary. Rolland

at first agreed, but much to Guilbeaux's disgust, he then
begged off, declaring that while he felt free to criticize
the French government on his own account, he could
not lend his name to an official Soviet publication
aimed at the French government: "All political intrigues
are repugnant to me." In the end, the work appeared in
Zurich, issued as the Promachos Verlag's only French
language volume, with an introduction by Platten, who
knew no French.[11]

The operation of Russische Nachrichten cost a
great deal of money. Most of the manuscripts sent from
Russia for publication were written in Russian, and the
agency had to develop its own stable of translators,
usually paying three hundred fifty to four hundred
francs for each work. The final copies in turn sold for a
variety of prices, which in sum did not cover costs; the
agency obviously required heavy subsidization.

In a typical example, Trotsky's *Arbeit, Disziplin
und Ordnung,* besides the cost of translation, was
printed in a run of 3000 copies at a cost of 1175 francs.
The book cost one franc in a book store for the casual
customer. The store owner in turn paid 60 centimes per
copy in cash, or if he sold the volume on a commission
basis, 70 centimes. In a letter of September 24, Reich
notified Platten that Russische Nachrichten could offer
this book at a group rate for workers' organizations—20
centimes per copy, to be resold at 40 centimes. As of
October 1, 2125 copies had been sold altogether.
Lenin's *Staat und Revolution* cost 8800 francs for its
run of 4000 copies; the book sold for four francs in
stores, returning just two francs per copy to Russische
Nachrichten when handled on a cash basis.[12]

The third aspect of Russische Nachrichten's activity, the survey of the European press, involved marking
and clipping articles, either for filing or for dispatching
to Moscow. One employee had the specific task of

keeping a card file of major articles in *Izvestiia*, the official organ of the Soviet government, for reference by the staff. The personnel hired for this work typified both the international atmosphere of Switzerland and the varied background of the internationalists who rallied to the support of the Bolshevik revolution.

Edmondo Peluso, whom Lenin had recommended to Berzin as a talented and prolific writer, had become an active participant in the Zimmerwald movement in 1915 and 1916 and had served as a member of the International Socialist Commission in Bern and as a delegate to the Kiental conference.[13] Peluso offered his services to the Soviet mission in July, and in response Berzin suggested that he work for Russische Nachrichten. Peluso apparently felt that this was less than he deserved, but he nevertheless accepted the job at a pay of 500 francs per month. Thereafter he reported to Reich rather than to Berzin.[14]

Peluso's earlier career confused even his contemporaries. He has been called both an Italian and a Portuguese. By his own testimony, he was born in Naples in 1882, but during the First World War he possessed an American passport. The coming of war found him in Vienna, where he was working as a correspondent of the Parisian socialist newspaper *L'Humanité*. He came to Switzerland in 1915 and enrolled for the summer semester at the University of Zurich; in the fall he moved to Geneva and wrote for the British newspaper *The Daily Citizen*. He taught Spanish for a while, worked as a translator, and then took a job with the Ukrainian Information Bureau in Lausanne, eventually becoming Assistant Director at a salary of 350 francs per month.[15]

Peluso's work for the Ukrainian bureau added complications in evaluating his career, since the bureau's director, Vladimir Stepankovsky, was a double—if not a triple—agent, maintaining ties with German, Austrian, and French officials. A Russian citizen, Stepankovsky had lived in London until the beginning of the war and had then moved to Vienna. In the summer of 1915 he had come to Lausanne and had established contact with the German mission in Bern, from which he began to receive subsidies. He had probably met Peluso in Austria, and in February 1916 he was able to give the Germans a detailed report, based on information from Peluso, on the activities of the International Socialist Commission.[16] More curious still was a memorandum which he submitted to the Swiss government in March 1918 and in which he declared, on the basis of reports from Peluso, that Angelica Balabanova was sending Bolshevik money into Switzerland from Stockholm.[17]

Peluso's weekly activity reports to the Russische Nachrichten documented his contribution to the revolutionary cause. On August 2 he sent two copies of Fritz Adler's brochure *Why I Killed Count Stürgkh* to Cesar Nogueira, secretary of the Socialist Party of Portugal, and he requested a summary of the current political situation in Portugal. He also promised to send news reports to the Portuguese socialist press, most of which eventually proved to have been taken from the releases of Russische Nachrichten. On August 4 Peluso wrote in a similar fashion to Pablo Inglesias, leader of the Spanish Socialist Party. On August 6 and 7 he sent Adler's brochure to French dissidents and to Ramsay Mac-Donald and Philip Snowden in England.[18]

On August 9 Peluso sent an article on Portugal for use in the *Russische Nachrichten;* on August 13 he sent the *Manchester Guardian* and the *Labour Leader* a translation of an article from the *Berner Tagwacht*, "Towards the Catastrophe." On August 15 he sent to *Socialista*, Madrid, an article on the Soviet Russian constitution; in his report Peluso insisted that *Socialista* had up to now depended on *L'Humanité* in Paris for its news on Russia. The same article on the constitution went to Enrique Dickmann in Buenos Aires. Peluso later claimed that his material had appeared in *Le Populaire*, *La Sentinelle*, and *Le Droit du peuple*. In December 1918, his work in Switzerland done, he was to make his way to Bavaria, carrying a letter of recommendation from Fritz Platten to Kurt Eisner.

Russische Nachrichten's Italian correspondent had just as mixed a background, and an even more complicated role than Peluso's. Isaak Schweide, born in Argentina in 1890, spoke both Russian and Italian, and his contemporaries considered him a German. In his past he had had connections with Willi Münzenberg and the Jungburschen in Zurich as well as with Angelica Balabanova and the Italian socialists. At one time he had served as secretary of the Italian Socialist Party in Switzerland. In 1917 he had traveled to Scandinavia, but the following year the International Socialist Commission in Stockholm dispatched him to Switzerland to report on Italian affairs as well as on Spain and America. Once back in the country, he established contact with Liubarsky, the mission's Italian specialist, and at the end of August he settled in Ascona, in Italian Switzerland, apparently as the successor to Baruch Lipnitsky.

Schweide's reports, addressed to Reich at the Russische Nachrichten but actually intended for Pokrovskaia, carried intimations of far reaching activities. (He signed them with the pseudonym "Ivanov Sovetskii.") He distributed Russische Nachrichten's various publications, and he regularly offered Reich new addresses for the daily bulletins. He also provided news.

In order to disguise his relationship with the Bolsheviks, Schweide instructed Reich, or Pokrovskaia, to send his "honorarium" to Dr. Anna Schweide in Ascona with a statement that the money came from her parents.

When the Soviet Red Cross opened its offices in Switzerland, Schweide declared that sending this money would be much easier.

Writing on September 4, Schweide stated that "the postal route into Italy is completely open for me." It might even be possible "to send a comrade there. No one must know of this." The call for secrecy was symptomatic of Schweide's difficulties. In a letter of August 19, after acknowledging the receipt of "goods" by courier, which he would send on "to our store," he added, "I ask you again to inform *absolutely no one* about my clients and about my possibility of sending goods." On September 16 he sent a long complaint about his problems: "I find myself here in such a situation that sometimes I have to divide myself into several parts in order to decide some questions." His responsibilities were great, and "despite my fourteen year party life, I would gladly divide this responsibility." In the face of all this, he lamented, the people in Bern were making still more trouble for him.

An Italian comrade, Schweide complained, had come illegally into the Ticino and had approached him for help in returning to Italy: "He does this with a commission from your official representatives."[19] Furthermore, Misiano, for whom Schweide protested his personal friendship, was recounting to everyone "in secret" his conversations with Liubarsky: "See what kind of nonsense comes out despite the fact that I warned both you and comrade L. against the Italian 'children.' " Misiano had now agreed to write articles for *Pravda,* insisting that Liubarsky had asked him to do so, and "every damn day I receive letters from this comrade in which he asks me how and what to write. Naturally I had to answer that this is none of my business. Tell me, please, you and comrade L., how can I continue to work quietly under such circumstances?" Liubarsky should warn Misiano that he is being careless, that Italian comrades in Basel, Zurich and Geneva were gossiping about his relations with the mission: "I ask only that you not use my name in this, since he, as a good Italian, can give this a personal character."

Despite such tribulations, however, Schweide was exultant about the course of his work. In concluding his lament of September 16, he declared, "The way, which had proved simpler than we thought, is completely open." On October 1 he simply requested, "Send me, please, in the next few days, several kilos of literature in French since I can sent it into Italy."[20]

In all, Schweide's Italian operation represented the major thrust of the activity of the Russische Nachrichten, despite the fact, as Lenin complained, that the agency produced little in the Italian language. (On September 29 Pageot reported that the Bolsheviks were attempting "to create in Switzerland the bases of a great Bolshevik movement in Italy.") Operating through Italians in Switzerland as well as through direct contacts in Italy, the Bolsheviks found that country their most vulnerable target among the Allied countries. On the other hand, France seems to have been Henri Guilbeaux's territory; Russische Nachrichten did little in this direction, and even the French language *Nouvelles de Russie* seemed an inferior publication compared to its German counterpart.

At the same time, however, the Bolsheviks did not limit themselves to any particular countries; they struck out in any direction which seemed opportune. At one point, Shklovsky directed Reich to forward a newspaper to Hungary, but to put as the sender "any name, but not an official institution."

In order to carry out Lenin's directive to avoid the charge of propaganda, the mission had established Russische Nachrichten as its cover agency, but as time went by it also added other information agencies. The Russian Telegraph Agency (ROSTA) pursued a more modest program, employing a staff of just two persons. Berzin's wife Rosa served as director; she had previous journalistic experience in Russia. ROSTA only collected news for transmittal to Russia; it had particular interest in reports from the French, English, and Italian press concerning developments in Siberia and Archangel, since, in Reich's words, "no direct news from there is said to have been reaching the Russian press." The mission considered expanding ROSTA's activity, but it had no time to do so.

Berzina's deputy, Jules Wetzosol (Vecezols), would seem to have played a more significant role than just that of news correspondent. A Latvian, he had studied in Zurich from 1905 to 1909 and had then gone to the United States. After returning in 1911 he had settled in Davos for reasons of health, but in 1915 he moved to Zurich. In 1917 he tried vainly to work for a prisoner of war relief agency, and during this time he made a name for himself as a radical. He was one of the elite group concerned with Holzmann's arrival in February 1918; Guilbeaux sent him a telegram concerning Holzmann's itinerary.

Like many others, Wetzosol applied to Platten for help in finding work, declaring, in a letter of April 4, 1918, "I have been a supporter of the Bolshevik line since 1904, I have also been in the ranks of the Bolsheviks abroad, I have been commissioned with special missions by leading Bolsheviks." In the summer of 1918 he went to work for ROSTA, and in the fall he served as the contact man in Bern for Russian civilians seeking aid either through the Soviet mission or through the Soviet Red Cross. He also maintained connections within the Latvian colony in Switzerland; his wife, a Swiss, worked as a typist for Reich.[21]

The mission also maintained a Russian Information Bureau within its own organization. Founded by Zamiatin, the bureau had a rather unclear mandate but a remarkable staff, including a Swiss and a Serb. The Swiss, Fritz Übersax, had once been a teacher of Shklovsky's oldest daughter and had become an intimate of the family. In 1918 Shklovsky offered him a job at first 400 francs and later 500 francs per month; Übersax had only been earning 200 francs per month as a teacher. He later told Swiss authorities that his job had consisted simply in searching Swiss newspapers for articles on political and economic affairs.[22]

A more intriguing figure was Ilia Milkich, born in Belgrade in 1884. Long active in the Serbian Socialist Party—he had represented it in 1910 at the conference of the Second International in Copenhagen and at this time had met Trotsky—Milkich had come to Switzerland in 1916 from Paris. He lived first in Geneva and then Zurich before settling in Bern. At the end of 1916, on doctor's advice, he moved to Davos, where he stayed until the summer of 1918. Accompanying him through all this was his mistress, Jeanne Jacob. (His wife and family still lived in Belgrade.)

Milkich had eagerly participated in Swiss radical movements. At the Swiss Socialist Party's special conference on the military question in June 1917, he had spoken in opposition to the idea of defense of the fatherland. After the Bolshevik revolution, he had written to the well-known Serbian radical Triša Kaclerovič, then in Stockholm working for the I.S.C., asking about the possibility of financial support. Kaclerovič responded by pointing to the Bolsheviks' decision to support radical movements, and he suggested that Milkich apply to the Soviet mission in Bern. Milkich received similar advice when he applied to Ernst Nobs; Nobs noted that the Soviet mission "surely needs numerous personnel," and told Milkich to use him and Platten as references.[23]

Swiss police noted that in March 1918 Milkich, then still in Davos, sought to collect the addresses of all Serbian workers in Switzerland; he was thought to have some money to distribute. A Davos police report of April 19 spoke of Milkich as a "simple, quiet man," who was always behind in his rent; on July 30, however, the same police agency called him "one of the most dangerous agitators for a general strike," and reported that he maintained a heavy correspondence with Stockholm.

At the end of July Milkich moved to Bern to take up his job with the Russian Information Bureau. (Jeanne Jacob became a translator.) As he told Swiss officials later, he had simply visited the mission and had received a job upon asking. He claimed that his work had consisted simply in reading the Yugoslav and the French press, but in 1919 he was to serve as the representative of Serbia at the founding congress of the Communist International.[24]

The activity of the three information agencies testified to the Bolsheviks' belief in the power of the word and also to their need for information about socialist movements in other countries. Fritz Platten had considered yet another press bureau and publishing house in Zurich, employing six or seven translators, but this idea died stillborn. On the other hand, while the distribution of literature and the collection of information required a high degree of organization, there is little evidence of the formation or development of definite plans for revolution. The Bolsheviks were attempting to stir revolutionary feelings in the West; they were not directing revolutions.[25]

8: THE GUILBEAUX AFFAIR

Of all the employees and contacts of the Soviet mission, Henri Guilbeaux drew the most fire from the authorities and from the press in Switzerland. He himself made no secret of his friendships with well-known revolutionaries: "As for the collaboration with Bolsheviks and Russian internationalists and more especially with Lenin, Trotsky, Lunacharsky, Balabanova and Radek, I glory in it, and I flatter myself that they have long shown me their confidence."[1] At the same time, to the discomfiture of his revolutionary friends, he made no secret of his contacts with known German agents. Declaring that his interest was the ending of the war, Guilbeaux averred that he felt free to discuss world affairs with anyone.

After the French government had convicted Guilbeaux in absentia of "dealing with the enemy," its mission in Bern watched his activity still more closely. The new French Minister to Switzerland, Paul Dutasta, and the Military Attaché, Colonel Pageot, embodied the antipathy which the French Prime Minister, Georges Clemenceau, felt for all "defeatist" elements, and for them Guilbeaux personified these elements.[2]

Pageot lost no opportunity to impress Bern with the threat which Guilbeaux posed. The French wanted to see him deported, or at least silenced. Ironically, the formal charge lodged against him in France proved self-defeating in Switzerland. The Bundesrat, acting in an analogous fashion to its decisions in the case of Willi Münzenberg, could not deport an alien to a country where he faced certain imprisonment or even execution. In such clashes between upholding their neutrality and maintaining the right of asylum, the Swiss, while gravely concerned about their own internal security, tended to give priority to the traditional right of asylum. The Swiss accepted, even solicited, Pageot's reports, but, as the attaché complained, they gave him little in return. Swiss authorities had carefully documented Guilbeaux's relations with Holzmann in February; they had a general idea of his role in the Zimmerwald movement; and the Swiss police recorded several meetings between Guilbeaux and German agents. They even claimed that Guilbeaux met in June with an agent of Alexander Parvus-Helphand, but they never developed any evidence that these two men were working together. When more Bolshevik emissaries began to arrive, the Swiss carefully noted their contacts with Guilbeaux, in each case reporting a transfer of money—the reports mentioned 10,000 francs with remarkable consistency—which Guilbeaux then allegedly used either for *Demain* or *La Nouvelle Internationale,* or even possibly sent on to France.

Guilbeaux defended himself publicly. In May he published a pamphlet in response to the charges of the Clemenceau government. Entitled *Mon crime. Contre-attaque et offensive,* the work was dedicated "to the victims of all the imperialist and capitalist governments, and in particular to all those who, in Germany, courageously defend the principles of international socialism." Emphasizing his concern for peace, Guilbeaux argued that even Grimm and Hoffmann had done nothing wrong in their misfortune of the previous year. In the aftermath of the Brest-Litovsk agreement, the program of the Zimmerwald movement could endorse any action for peace, taken in conjunction with the nationals of any country.[3]

Guilbeaux's activities in fact seemed to be aimed exclusively toward the dissemination of antiwar propaganda, spiced by his sympathetic views of the Bolshevik revolution. What organizational activities he undertook appear to have concerned the distribution of publications rather than any preparations for revolutionary upheavals. Since this fell clearly within the traditional conceptions of political asylum, the Swiss found it difficult to deal with the case; eventually they settled on attempting to determine the factors which motivated Guilbeaux—was he sincere or was he just a paid agent of a foreign power?

Clemenceau's campaign against Guilbeaux had charged him with being a German agent. As Bolshevik activity in Switzerland developed in the course of 1918, Pageot made a rather easy transition to charging Guilbeaux with being a Russian agent or even a Russo-German agent. Guilbeaux's own actions and statements only served to convince Pageot that his charges were correct; the Swiss expressed more concern about attempting to understand his motives.

Just as Holzmann and Zalkind had taken steps immediately to meet Guilbeaux upon their arrival in Switzerland, so too did Berzin quickly establish contact. According to Guilbeaux's memoirs, Berzin's secretary, Maurice Leiteisen, came to Geneva with an invitation for Guilbeaux to come to Bern. Since Berzin had already retired to Sigriswyl, Guilbeaux had to travel to the Lake of Thun to find him. The two had never met before, and according to Guilbeaux, Berzin "gave me greetings and salutations from Lenin, informed himself of my activity, of my work with the review *Demain*, and with the situation in France."[4] Berzin also informed Guilbeaux that henceforth his dispatches to *Pravda* should be sent through the Soviet mission in Bern rather than through Stockholm.

In the succeeding weeks, Guilbeaux, again working in Geneva, maintained a vigorous correspondence with

Zalkind and Leiteisen. Zalkind kept Guilbeaux informed of his plans to come to Geneva in the vain attempt to take over the Russian consulate on June 20. On June 19, Berzin sent Guilbeaux a personal letter from Lenin and offered the courier service of the mission if he cared to answer.[5] Although Berzin promised to come to Geneva himself, he proved unable to make the trip.

On June 18 Colonel Pageot took Guilbeaux's case directly to the Swiss Bundesanwaltschaft and demanded action, warning that Guilbeaux posed a threat to Switzerland itself. The Swiss responded only that they would investigate the matter. Since the French had an arrest order outstanding against him, the Swiss could not deport Guilbeaux; they would welcome, however, any proof which Pageot would care to submit. In his report to the War Ministry, Pageot declared that he would undertake to prove Guilbeaux's culpability "as much as a revolutionary agent as a hireling of Germany."[6]

On June 20 Pageot returned with his formal charge, contained in a memorandum on Bolshevik activities in Switzerland. Discussing the activities of Holzmann, Zalkind, and Lipnitsky, Pageot's memorandum circulated in many copies through the Swiss, the French, and even the British governments, and it served to influence the western attitude toward the Bolsheviks in Switzerland throughout the following months, again and again being echoed in reports and memoranda.

Pageot indicated that the Russians had organized a "Bolshevik propaganda bureau in Switzerland and in the neighboring countries." In Zurich, Zalkind was charged with revolutionizing German Switzerland; Baruch Lipnitsky, in Lausanne, concerned himself with Italy; and Guilbeaux in Geneva looked after French Switzerland and France. Zalkind was allegedly the treasurer of the operation. That Zalkind had already moved his headquarters to Bern at this time, and that Lipnitsky was to leave Lausanne on June 29 did not hinder western intelligence agents from repeating this table of organization over and over, treating it as current news even in November 1918. What apparently gave the report as a whole its impact was the astonishing assertion, subsequently admitted by Guilbeaux, that a German agent, Paul Schlesinger, had given money to underwrite the publication of *Demain*.

Schlesinger lived in Bern—indeed, in the same pension as Ilia Milkich and Jeanne Jacob—as a correspondent of the *Vossische Zeitung*, the organ of the German Catholic Zentrum party. In the spring of 1917 Guilbeaux told him of the financial straits of *Demain*. When Schlesinger offered to talk with other persons about the matter, Guilbeaux insisted that he would not take money from the German government. Schlesinger then contacted Jacques Gabriel von Rosenberg, a wealthy emigré from Russia then living in St. Moritz. Guilbeaux declared that the publication of *Demain* cost about 1000 francs per month, his own expenses included; Schlesinger and Rosenberg reached agreement on a figure of 10,000-12,000 francs as an annual subvention, plus 350 francs per month for Guilbeaux personally.

In response to the questions of Swiss authorities, Schlesinger insisted that he had taken an interest in Guilbeaux's work "only because of his general personal political outlook which he manifested as a Zimmerwaldist." Schlesinger denied any socialist sympathies of his own and insisted that only after the agreement had been made did Guilbeaux make his transition to Bolshevism. Schlesinger estimated that he had in fact passed on no more than 1800 francs.

Rosenberg, born in Zhitomir in 1858, freely admitted giving money to Guilbeaux, although he could not remember how much: "It could be several thousand, in order to bring about peace." Rosenberg explained, "Unfortunately I have relatives in both hostile camps and I want to work for peace with all the means at my command." Claiming to be a Ukrainian, he insisted that he had not previously met Guilbeaux, whom Schlesinger had identified as a man "who is struggling for peace," and that in all he had spoken with Guilbeaux "only three times for a few minutes."[7] A British report, on the other hand, identified Rosenberg as a member of a group long seeking a separate peace between Germany and Russia, and Rosenberg may well have been the individual, "a Rosenthal, or however the fellow in St. Moritz is called," who approached Robert Grimm with a request for the address of the Bolsheviks and of Angelica Balabanova.[8]

In his memoirs, Guilbeaux admitted taking the money, and in the fall of 1918, when the charges became public, he spoke freely of the matter to his friends. In accepting the money, he argued, he had simply sought aid from any sympathetic camp: "I have submitted to no order, to no directive, to no indication, and I remained the absolute master of my review."[9] Nevertheless the fact that he had received money through German channels proved decisive in Pageot's campaign against Guilbeaux.

On June 28 Pageot delivered another memorandum to the Swiss, claiming that Zalkind had personally delivered money to Guilbeaux on his several visits to Geneva. On each of two occasions, he had allegedly handed over 10,000 francs "destined to be sent to French defeatists." Reusing the amounts which he had once claimed that Lipnitsky had given Guilbeaux, Pageot also declared that Zalkind had paid 2000 francs for the publication of *Demain* and *La Nouvelle Internationale*. As encouragement for the Swiss to move against Guilbeaux, Pageot concluded by noting that Guilbeaux kept all his papers in his apartment, "in a strongbox and in a desk."[10]

On July 9 the Federal Government directed Geneva police to arrest Guilbeaux and to search his home. Citing reports that Guilbeaux had taken money from Zalkind and from Schlesinger, the order declared that "Guilbeaux's conduct should be considered as contrary to our neutrality and dangerous for our country." The Geneva authorities were also directed to arrest Gustave Noverraz, a publisher with whom Guilbeaux worked closely.[11] On July 11 the police carried out the order.

At the time of his arrest, Guilbeaux admitted taking money from Zalkind, but he asserted that this constituted payment for his work as a correspondent of *Pravda*. He denied sending any money on to France. He also admitted his agreement with Schlesinger. Writing from prison on July 12 he declared that he had never acted against the interests of Swiss neutrality. His had been "an active propaganda in favor of the peace of peoples," and he had pointed out, "in many cases, that the prolongation of the war could be harmful to Switzerland's neutrality." He signed his statement as a correspondent of *Pravda*.[12]

For the moment the Swiss brought no formal charges, while investigators rummaged through Guilbeaux's papers, discovering letters from Zalkind, Leiteisen, Berzin, and Lenin. (Because they could not read the signature, they failed to identify several revealing letters from Balabanova.) In the meantime, Guilbeaux sat in prison, unable to communicate even with his lawyer, Jacques Dicker. Dicker filed several complaints against this treatment, insisting that his client was ill, but only on August 3 did the authorities grant him permission to visit Guilbeaux, and then only in the presence of a guard. On August 5 Dicker objected to this condition and refused to see Guilbeaux.[13]

Following leads obtained from their search of Guil-

beaux's papers, Swiss authorities interviewed a number
of individuals. They took testimony from Paul Schlesinger on August 1 and again on August 3. Since Rosenberg
was traveling, they could speak to him only on August
8. When they caught up with Zalkind on August 13, the
Russian denied that he knew Guilbeaux and that he had
ever given him money. The police officer in charge of
the interrogation declared, "The answers of Jonas Zalkind to our repeated and exhaustive questions are so
curt, bitterly repelling and ironic, that one must strongly doubt their credibility. The manner and way in which
Zalkind responded to our detailed statements is so offensive that an arrest seems warranted."[14] The Federal
Justice Department, recalling that the Foreign Office
had repeatedly declared that Zalkind had not been registered as a member of the Soviet mission, concurred,
ordering Zalkind's arrest and charging him with falsely
representing himself as an envoy of the Soviet government. Within an hour of the police action, Shklovsky
was on the phone protesting to Paravicini, who embar-
rassedly recalled that Berzin had indeed sent notification of Zalkind's nomination as consul general. At Paravicini's request, the police immediately released Zalkind.

Four days earlier, on August 9, the police had had
the same experience with Anatole Divilkovsky. Their
investigation into Guilbeaux's affairs had given them
evidence on Divilkovsky's close association with Guilbeaux and at the same time it had implicated Divilkovsky in the Zurich "bomb affair" of April 1918. Divilkovsky had allegedly concealed Toni Waibel for several
days while the latter was fleeing the Zurich police who
were investigating that case. (Zurich police also tended
to implicate Zalkind in the affair.) Viewing Divilkovsky
as an emigré without special privileges, the Swiss ordered his arrest; Shklovsky immediately came to Paravicini with the complaint that Divilkovsky was in fact a

functionary of the mission, working for the press section. On this occasion, too, Paravicini yielded, and the Political Department ordered Divilkovsky's release. To the relief of all concerned, Divilkovsky left for Russia in October.[15]

Guilbeaux's arrest also brought a thunder of protests from the Swiss left. Romain Rolland published an open letter in his support. *La Sentinelle* linked Guilbeaux's case with that of Luigi Bertoni, an Italian anarchist then sitting in prison, as glaring examples of police repression; Paul Graber, the editor of *La Sentinelle*, described the working class as caught between revolutionary adventures and bourgeois reactions. Graber's colleague, Humbert-Droz, rallied more enthusiastically to Guilbeaux, questioning whether his arrest did not put into question the independence of the Swiss police from foreign influences.[16] On August 16 the newspaper carried a letter from the noted Swiss scientist Auguste Forel, protesting the Swiss government's refusal to allow Dicker to see Guilbeaux alone. Guilbeaux, Forel wrote, was "a perfectly honest man, though too extreme and too violent in his writings."

Writing in the *Berner Tagwacht* of July 18, Robert Grimm demanded an explanation for Guilbeaux's arrest. If the government considered him implicated in the Zurich bomb affair, it should present its evidence. Guilbeaux was released on August 12, without any formal charges being filed; the next day, Grimm declared that the Swiss government had failed to find any evidence against him. He also repeated the charges that Guilbeaux had been mistreated in prison.[17]

The Soviet mission trod its ground carefully during Guilbeaux's imprisonment. Its Dutch employee, Herman Gorter, prepared an article protesting the arrest, but Berzin advised him against publishing it. Gorter then decided to withhold it since, as he explained to Guilbeaux, "The Russians above all have more experience than I on this point."[18]

The anti-Bolshevik forces in Switzerland looked approvingly on the turmoil caused by Guilbeaux's arrest. An appeal for funds by *La Nouvelle Internationale* was taken as a sign that a key link in the chain of revolutionary funds had been removed. Pageot claimed to have intercepted a letter from a Bolshevik group in Geneva: "The Geneva bureau, charged with correspondence relative to the affairs of France, had not been able to function in view of the incarceration of the director of *Demain*."[19] *Demain* did not appear in August 1918.

Like Grimm, Guilbeaux thought that his release meant that the Swiss government was essentially admitting its failure to develop a case against him. In fact, the government now charged the Bundesanwaltschaft, the federal Attorney General, with drawing up an indictment against Guilbeaux. Pageot attributed the decision to pursue the case to the Minister of Justice, Eduard Müller, who, ironically, had repeatedly been the target of charges of Germanophilism. Pageot confidently informed Paris that he had the ear of the man charged with preparing a general report.[20]

Brazen as his activities might have been, Guilbeaux manifested no greater a sense of caution after his release. Declaring himself "exhausted by the five weeks of stupid incarceration," he retreated to the Lake of Thun for a vacation. Heartened by the congratulations of wellwishers, he stopped in Bern on the way to report to Zalkind and Liubarsky. Then settling near Berzin's residence in Sigriswyl, Guilbeaux even made a visit to Schlesinger, who was staying in Spiess on the other side of the lake.[21] He met frequently with Berzin and Zalkind, with whom he took walks. On these occasions, Zalkind "diverted us by his spirit, his droll reflections and his aphorisms. He hardly considered plotting against the Federal Government, but the Swiss politicians were a frequent theme on which we exercised our irony and our humor."[22]

Behind Guilbeaux came the French agents. Pageot at this time perceived an unusual movement of socialists into the Bernese Highlands: Pieter Troelstra from Holland, Carl Legien and Philipp Scheidemann from Germany, Solomon Grumbach from France. From August 26 to August 30 meetings took place in Interlaken and Lucerne between these men, reportedly discussing the possibility of another international conference. Pageot placed Guilbeaux in the middle of these developments as a representative of the French Zimmerwald movement.[23]

On August 31, a Sunday, Guilbeaux called upon Berzin in Sigriswyl only to find the envoy and his wife both prostrate with grief. In a weak voice, Berzin explained that he had just received news of the attempt on Lenin's life; the telegram had indicated that Lenin's condition was grave. (The first news reports, published in the next day's Swiss newspapers, said to the contrary that Lenin was in no danger.) The next day Guilbeaux called again only to hear that Lenin's condition was still serious. Only several days later was the group relieved to hear of Lenin's recovery.[24]

In the meantime, the Bundesanwaltschaft completed its work; on August 21 it filed its report with the Justice Department and on the 28th the report was sent on to the Bundesrat. In considering the crucial question as to whether Guilbeaux was only following the dictates of his conscience, the report pointed to Guilbeaux's admitted contacts with German agents and concluded that he was nothing more than a revolutionary mercenary, a paid agent for the Bolsheviks, issuing propaganda directed against Swiss institutions. The report recom-

mended his expulsion from the country. Because of the
complication of the criminal charges against Guilbeaux
in France, however, the Bundesrat put off taking any
action for the time being.[25]

In the course of September, the details of the
Bundesanwaltschaft's report leaked out to the press,
especially to the pro-government newspapers such as
Der Bund and *Die Neue Zürcher Zeitung.* Much as they
wanted to defend Guilbeaux, the socialists were thunderstruck by the news of the Schlesinger affair. Stories
of the venality of the bourgeois press were legion in
Switzerland; socialist publications were supposed to
have impeccable credentials. At the Kiental conference
in 1916, the Italian representatives had forced Herman
Greulich, the patriarch of Swiss socialism, to leave the
meeting because he had served as a channel for an offer
of money from an American pacifist to support antiwar
propaganda among Italian socialists. Guilbeaux's conduct forced the socialists to reconsider their posture,
and the resulting controversy created a new touchstone
of the sympathies of Swiss Socialists for the Soviet
government.

The *Berner Tagwacht,* as late as September 20, had
still unreservedly come to Guilbeaux's defense, calling
for united socialist action against his expulsion and
insisting that he had done nothing criminal or in violation of Swiss neutrality. A week later, on the twenty-
seventh, the newspaper summarized the Schlesinger
case, without challenging the motives of Schlesinger or
Rosenberg. Even while still accepting the thought that
the money was meant only to support pacifist aims, it
could see only "a gross mistake." The newspaper sol-
emnly declared that it could not pass judgment on the
case; the Socialist Party would have to consider it formally.

Grimm obviously felt that Guilbeaux had embarrassed the socialist cause. On September 28 the *Berner Tagwacht* published a sharp attack on the theory being advanced in some western circles that German money was flowing into the Bolshevik coffers to support revolutionary movements in the Entente countries. Guilbeaux's actions had offered credence to just such assertions.

In *La Sentinelle* of September 27, Paul Graber came out much more forcefully in criticism of Guilbeaux. Recalling that he had criticized Grimm the previous year and expressing the conviction that in Grimm's case there had been no question of German money, Graber called Guilbeaux's action "an unpardonable imprudence" but not treason. Fortunately, he went on to say, Guilbeaux "is playing no role in the Swiss workers' movement and is only an intermediary for ideas in the international movement."

On October 1 the Bundesrat considered the case and judged Guilbeaux guilty of "relations" with the Russian Bolsheviks. It chose, however, neither to expel nor to imprison him; instead it treated him essentially as it would a Swiss citizen under similar circumstances and ordered him to leave Geneva for some area in the interior of the country. If he did not cease his propaganda activity, however, he might yet be expelled.[26]

The Swiss Socialist Party, which would normally leap eagerly to the defense of any socialist persecuted by the government, found itself deeply split. Graber became more and more critical. In Bern Grimm proclaimed that he would make no judgment, and under the circumstances this represented a repudiation of Guilbeaux. (Guilbeaux characterized Grimm's stance as "moderate in tone but not without rancour.")[27] Ernst Nobs and the Zurich party defended him. *Volksrecht* of October 4 ridiculed the Bundesrat's decision: "Dear heaven, who then does not stand in some relation to 'the revolutionary Russian Bolsheviks.' " Faced by such division, the party empaneled a special commission consisting of Graber, Platten, Studer, Hans Vogel, and Charles Naine, with Zalkind participating as the representative of the Bolshevik mission. Within socialist circles, the affair quickly became a direct conflict between Guilbeaux and Graber; since the Bolsheviks rallied to Guilbeaux's support, the affair also became a test of loyalty toward the revolution in Russia. Within the special commission, Guilbeaux launched a bitter counterattack, charging Graber with seeking vengeance for a longstanding dispute over personalities contributing to *La Sentinelle*. Graber responded in the columns of his newspaper, publicly challenging Guilbeaux's right even to call himself a socialist. Guilbeaux, Graber asserted, was "much more an impatient individualist than a socialist." Guilbeaux's supporters in Geneva, calling themselves the International Socialist Group, used *La Nouvelle Internationale* to speak of the "Graber affair" as an answer to Graber's discussion of the "Guilbeaux affair."[28]

When news of the dispute reached Moscow, Lenin reacted strongly, even criticizing Berzin for not reacting vigorously enough: "I see that Graber and Grimm have attacked Guilbeaux stupidly and foully. How could you see anything bad in his taking money? *I do not understand.* One cannot censure a valuable comrade without *formal* examination of the case!? Who of the *members of the party* (named by you) has examined the matter? No one! But from Guilbeaux's facts and from the decision of the Geneva commission [probably the International Socialist Group] the case is clearer than clear *for* Guilbeaux."[29]

Lenin linked the Guilbeaux case with that of Jakob Herzog, who at this time was expelled from the Socialist Party in Zurich. On September 30 bank employees in

Zurich had gone out on strike, and workers' groups had expanded this into a local general strike. Although the Zurich Workers' Union attempted to call off the strike on the evening of October 1, restless spirits, led by Herzog, insisted on continuing the struggle. In an effort to enforce strike discipline, the Socialist Party excluded Herzog, and he responded on October 6 by founding a Communist Party. (The members of Herzog's group eventually became known as the "Old Communists," in distinction to the "New Communists" who only later split off from the left wing of the Swiss Socialist Party.)[30]

Lenin immediately expressed his support for Herzog. In a letter of October 15 he directed Berzin, "Especially give my greetings to Guilbeaux and Herzog." On October 25 he stated, "What is the story with Herzog's exclusion? I think that we must speak out *for* him. The excluders are scum, opportunists. Write about it. I hope that you have liquidated the Guilbeaux 'affair' in the sense that they have fully rehabilitated him. Give him my greetings. Where is he?"[31]

Berzin later claimed that Lenin had been misinformed about his attitudes toward Guilbeaux: "During all this period I was a zealous defender of comrade Guilbeaux not only against the Swiss opportunists but equally against the ex-communist Balabanova."[32] Guilbeaux in turn believed in the loyalty of both Berzin and Zalkind, but the mission generally acted cautiously. The Soviet government added its own formal support by granting Guilbeaux honorary Soviet citizenship and by naming him a member of the newly established Academy of Social Sciences. Whether voluntarily or only on Lenin's orders, Berzin now did what he could to rally Swiss opinion behind Guilbeaux.

Ironically, Graber had at one time had the reputation of being pro-Bolshevik. Pageot still believed that he was taking subsidies from the Bolsheviks, although he admitted that "Graber's role in this case is not absolutely certain."[33] Graber's alienation from the Bolsheviks, probably influenced to a degree by Alexander Shreider, had been developing gradually. From Berzin's point of view this also raised problems of maintaining a sympathetic press in Western Switzerland. *La Sentinelle* had served as a valuable outlet, and Berzin was loathe to let it go.

Jules Humbert-Droz, Graber's colleague on the editorial board of the newspaper, had repeatedly declared his support of proletarian revolution; now his differences with Graber grew as he insisted that Guilbeaux was more a victim than a culprit. In mid-October, Humber-Droz visited Berzin and informed him of his inclination to quit the editorial board. Berzin attempted to dissuade him, pointing out that Graber would then have his own way with the paper and the revolution would have lost a valuable organ. If Humbert-Droz nevertheless chose to leave, Berzin indicated that the Soviet mission was willing to purchase another newspaper—he suggested one in Lausanne—which it would then turn over to him. In the end, Humbert-Droz decided to remain with *La Sentinelle*, and on October 23, after a long absence, his name returned as a byline on the front page.[34]

For all the controversy, Guilbeaux still did not change his ways. Pageot, hopefully but mistakenly, reported on October 23, "Guilbeaux's influence in Switzerland has been definitively compromised," but Guilbeaux continued to meet with Germans, Russians, and French alike. He indicated to Swiss authorities that in compliance with the Bundesrat's order he would settle in the canton of Appenzell in Eastern Switzerland, but he made no move to do so. The hectic events of the end of October and November found him still in Geneva, publishing *Demain*.

In seeking a friendly press, it should be noted, the Soviet mission had acted no differently than the missions of the capitalist governments. Both the Germans and the British invested heavily in particular newspapers. For the Swiss socialists, however, this practice had seemed repugnant. Ernst Nobs in Zurich repeatedly proclaimed his newspaper's purity, and Friedrich Schneider, editor of *Vorwärts* in Basel, claimed to have refused money from the Soviet mission. For Guilbeaux, such considerations seemed irrelevant.

9: THE SPECTRE OF REVOLUTION

By the end of October, Allied representatives in Switzerland looked on the activity of the Bolsheviks with great concern, and they complained bitterly of the tolerance which the Swiss government displayed toward the various revolutionary elements in the country. The French military attaché accused the Bundesrat of weakness and pusillanimity, and he spoke with scorn of the concern of the Swiss for their investments in Russia. He also expressed the opinion that the Swiss expected the revolutionaries to leave the country once the war had ended; therefore, the Bundesrat chose simply to postpone taking any definite action. The English seemed more restrained in their comments. The counsellor of the legation, Lord Acton, spoke disdainfully of how the "elderly and the timorous in Switzerland have long trembled in their shoes" at the thought that Lenin was seeking to foment "a Bolshevik revolution in this country." Rumbold, on the other hand, treated the Bolsheviks more seriously, although he agreed with Acton that the Germans stood behind the revolutionary agitation.[1]

On October 27 Colonel Pageot, in his weekly summary of Swiss affairs, declared that public opinion "is beginning to be disturbed for Switzerland itself by the Bolshevik plots." A week later he saw the situation as still more threatening: "The great preoccupation of opinion at the present time is the fear of Bolshevik plots which are demonstrating extraordinary activity in Switzerland." The government, however, was only continuing in its "feeble" response.[2]

The event which most upset the Entente representatives, and which also galvanized the Swiss government

147

into action, was the arrival in Switzerland of Angelica Balabanova, the secretary of the International Socialist Commission. Ostensibly sent to work for the Russian Red Cross, Balabanova, by Berzin's own admission, never got around to this task. More likely was Platten's explanation, offered later, that Balabanova was working for the convocation of a new conference of Zimmerwald socialists. Balabanova's contacts with Italian socialists aroused the greatest fears on the part of the Entente.

Balabanova's arrival especially shocked the Swiss because the Political Department believed that it had already effectively blocked her from entering the country. On July 16 the Swiss consul in Stockholm received a telephone call from the Soviet mission there, asking what formalities had to be executed to obtain permission for a member of the mission to travel to Switzerland. Before answering, the consul insisted on knowing the name of the person in question; after some hesitation, the Russian caller revealed that it concerned in fact not a member of the mission, but rather Balabanova, who was to go to Switzerland as a courier.

The consul responded that in this case he must first have complete details about the trip, and he must furthermore be sure that the trip was absolutely essential. On July 20 he received a formal written request, stating that Balabanova "is betaking herself to Bern as a diplomatic courier of the People's Commissariat of Foreign Affairs." Thereupon he wrote to the Swiss Fremdenpolizei, the alien police, asking for instructions and noting that "insofar as is known to me, Frau Balabanova is a member of the Zimmerwald Socialist Commission here."[3]

In the meantime, the Russian mission in Stockholm took the delay to mean that the visa had been rejected, and it denied visas to two Swiss seeking to enter Russia. The consul anxiously asked his superiors in the Swiss mission in Berlin to help him obtain an answer from Bern.[4] The fact that the Swiss found it possible to enter Russia from Finland even without the visa from the mission in Stockholm did little to relieve his concern.

On July 28 the mission in Berlin asked the consul for more information, since Joffe had also stopped granting visas for Swiss couriers to Russia. The consul responded that the whole affair had seemed to him "an abuse of the designation 'diplomatic passport,' " and he had simply requested instructions of Bern while notifying the Russians of the reason for the delay. He had not, he insisted, denied the visa; he had only asked for a ruling from Bern.[5] Mercier thereupon wrote to Bern, "It seems that the Russians are attempting to bring all sorts of people by various ways into Switzerland under the cover of a courier." Would it not be possible, he questioned, to limit the courier service only to the stretch from Moscow through Berlin to Switzerland?[6]

The Swiss consul's original request for instructions had passed between the Political Department and the Fremdenpolizei for several days before the Political Department, on August 2, formally pronounced its decision to deny the visa. The practice, already confirmed in response to Joffe's demands in June, of not permitting couriers to be sent from mission to mission applied also in this case: "The coming of Frau Balabanova is moreover undesirable for us, so that we would want to block it in any case." Should Balabanova attempt to enter Switzerland with a regular visa, the Political Department wanted to be notified immediately. The matter now seemed settled, but the Swiss had not reckoned with Balabanova's traveling to Moscow to begin her journey.[7]

Unexpectedly, Balabanova entered Switzerland on October 16 and arrived in Zurich on the seventeenth. Two Italian socialists met her train. There ensued a

flurry of directives from Bern to local officials as well as
to the military intelligence, seeking to learn how Balabanova had managed to come; the government did not
even know whether she had come from Germany or
from Italy. On October 29 Shklovsky finally informed
the Political Department of her arrival with a diplomatic
passport. Since the secretary of the mission, Liubarsky,
was ill with the flu, however, Shklovsky was unable as
yet to deliver the document. The official purpose of her
visit was to effect the "reemigration of Russian soldiers
from France"; the Swiss consul in Berlin had duly visaed
her passport on October 14, probably remembering his
instructions in the Natanson case to give all diplomatic
agents visas without asking any questions or raising any
objections.

Despite all the attention which she received, however, Balabanova succeeded in concealing the nature of
her work; observers were left to their speculations.
Pageot complained that her activities "have in general
been surrounded by a certain mystery." The intelligence
services of both the Entente and the Central Powers
appeared convinced that she had carried ten million gold
rubles for distribution to revolutionaries; all seemed
agreed that Italy represented a major target; they tended
to disagree as to whether she also had a charge to work
in Germany or France. The French also believed that
Balabanova was investigating the possibility of bringing
the I.S.C. back to Switzerland.

On October 16, before he knew of Balabanova's
presence in Switzerland, Pageot reported on a meeting
in Geneva of Swiss internationalists, including Zalkind
and Guilbeaux, which had agreed to organize demonstrations in November in honor of the anniversary of the
Bolshevik revolution. The meeting had also agreed that
the internationalists needed Balabanova's personal aid in
Switzerland. A month earlier, Pageot had taken note of

a public polemic between Grimm and Balabanova, as the
Swiss socialist criticized the inactivity of the I.S.C. and
insisted that the organization should be returned to
Switzerland. Balabanova responded that this was a time
of action, not resolutions, but Pageot interpreted her
position as contemplating a return to Switzerland.[8]

According to Balabanova's memoirs, she herself
had originated the idea of her mission to Switzerland.
She allegedly suggested the trip to Lenin during a visit
to Moscow; her memoirs made no mention of her attempt to travel directly from Stockholm. The several
versions of her memoirs, moreover, offered different
accounts of her motivation. A German version, published in 1927, spoke of her desire "to inform myself
directly about the Zimmerwald movement in the West
and then to relax for a few days in Switzerland." In
another publication of 1928 she described her trip as
part of her work for the I.S.C. with the purpose of
"orientation" and of "entering into contact with various
Zimmerwald parties." An English version of 1938 explained her purpose as that "of re-establishing contacts
with my Italian friends and of becoming better ac-
quainted with the general European situation, particularly that of Italy." Another collection of reminiscences
of Lenin, published in 1964, spoke of her deciding on
her trip while still in Stockholm; disturbed by reports
from "trusted Italian comrades living in Zurich" about
Guilbeaux's dealings with Schlesinger, "I decided to
leave immediately for Switzerland to take action, if
necessary, toward Guilbeaux's expulsion from the Zimmerwald Movement."[9]

In her most detailed account of planning the trip,
the English version of 1938, Balabanova insisted that
Lenin advised her against the project. Nevertheless she
insisted, declaring that she would speak at no public
meetings and would indulge in no political activity: "In

two weeks I shall be back." In order to give an appearance of independence, she reminisced, "I wanted to be
independent of the Russian government and of our
embassy in Switzerland."[10]

In none of the versions did Balabanova mention
the idea of facilitating the "reemigration of Russian
soldiers in France." Her activity in Switzerland, moreover, in no way corresponded to the description of her
intentions which she claimed to have offered Lenin.
Least of all was she to be satisfied with a stay of just
two weeks, or less, if one considered travel time in her
estimate. If her memory of her discussion with Lenin
was correct, then either the task or the opportunities
which she found in Switzerland proved greater than she
expected. On the other hand, her variety of memoirs
may have been deliberately misleading.

Balabanova stayed in Zurich for three days, October 17 to 20, during which time she met most frequently with the Italians—Misiano, Visani, and
Sacerdote. She reportedly gave a sizable amount of
money to them to support the publication of *L'Avvenire del Lavoratore.* Her arrival in Zurich raised all the
more furor because it coincided with the public announcement of the verdict against Gino Andrei for his
role in the smuggling affair of January 1918. So intense
was the press discussion of her intentions in the country
at this time that the *Berner Tagwacht,* in a heavy-
handed attempt at humor, announced on October 23:
"Comrade Balabanova is now even in Switzerland herself, and the revolution in Italy will begin next Friday at
exactly twelve noon. On Monday it will then break
loose in Switzerland."

From October 20 to 23, Balabanova stayed at the
Volkshaus in Bern; according to French sources, she
spoke publicly every evening about the accomplishments of Bolshevik rule in Russia. During this time she

also conferred at length with members of the Soviet mission, although the intelligence reports could not specify with whom.[11]

Her activities over the next several days seem particularly obscure. Allied sources placed her on October 25 at a conference of revolutionaries on the Beatenberg, presumably at Berzin's residence. Whether such a conference actually took place is doubtful. Nevertheless, according to a widely circulated report—to be found in the French, the British, and the Swiss archives alike—the Bolshevik representatives met on the Beatenberg to consider directives first issued by a conference at the Soviet mission in Berlin under Joffe's direction; this meeting allegedly designated Switzerland "as the center of revolutionary propaganda for the countries of the Entente." Balabanova, who had indeed stopped to visit Joffe in Berlin, allegedly carried these directives to Switzerland, and the conference of October 25, attended by Platten, Balabanova and Natanson, selected Germany, Italy, and Hungary as states particularly ripe for revolution: "Switzerland has been designated as the residence of the revolutionary General Staff." Despite some misgivings about the anti-Bolshevik feelings of the French Swiss, the gathering also reportedly decided to proceed with the organization of revolution in Switzerland.[12]

The report of the meeting pandered to all the preconceptions of the Entente observers: the conviction that the Germans were encouraging the efforts of the Bolsheviks in Switzerland, the role assigned to Switzerland as the *place d'armes* of the socialist revolution, and, of course, the belief in the French Swiss as the main bulwark against Germanophilism and in the susceptibility of the German-speaking Swiss to Bolshevik ideas. Apart from the single document, many times repeated, however, there is no other evidence of the presence of any of the principals on the Beatenberg on

October 25 and 26. Natanson's presence at such a gathering, moreover, must be considered highly doubtful. Therefore, in the absence of independent corroborating evidence, this report offers far less on the question of Balabanova's activities than it does on the pattern of thinking of the observers attempting to follow her. The Entente representatives in Switzerland were convinced that the meeting had taken place as described.

Sometime during the last week of October, Balabanova traveled to Geneva to see Guilbeaux. According to a Swiss report, she took him 10,000 francs. More significant was a French report that Balabanova took a dislike to her French comrade on this occasion: "She does not seem to take very seriously the role of the latter in Switzerland and does not believe in his sincerity."[13] The antagonism between these two soon became legendary; in their respective memoirs, they attacked each other bitterly. Yet in the spring of 1918, contrary to Guilbeaux's memoirs, they were still on friendly terms.[14]

What turned Guilbeaux and Balabanova against each other at this point is not completely clear; perhaps Balabanova disapproved of Guilbeaux's lack of conspiratorial sense, of his willingness to be seen publicly with Germans, or of his lack of a firm ideology. In her memoirs she emphasized her shock over the Schlesinger affair.[15] At any rate, she seems to have foreseen Guilbeaux's stormy career earlier than most others, certainly earlier than Lenin did.

On her trip through western Switzerland, Balabanova also found time to stop in Fribourg, where she visited interned Russian soldiers. Although the visit was not generally noted by the Swiss press or by Entente agents, she made no effort to conceal her presence. In the evening she sat in the tavern "Tête noire" on the

Rue de Lausanne and spoke freely with all who cared to approach her.[16]

The end of October found Balabanova again in Zurich, working with the Italians. According to a report by Zurich police, she spoke at meetings at the Volkshaus on Helvetiaplatz and at the Cooperative Italiana, where she praised Soviet Russia and predicted that "it will be still better in Switzerland." Only revolution, she asserted, could extirpate militarism and capitalism. The police also reported that she had won the support of Herzog's Communist Party.[17]

There is conflicting testimony as to whether Balabanova visited Italian Switzerland. She was originally scheduled to visit Ascona on October 31, but on the 30th Reich sent word to Schweide that she could not come because of Liubarsky's illness. On the other hand, British reports placed her in Lugano for at least several hours, but on some unspecified day.[18]

By the end of October the Entente had become extremely nervous about Balabanova's activities. The imminent ending of the war, according to Pageot, offered only new dangers from this quarter; Platten had given a speech in La Chaux-de-Fonds depicting the possibilities of revolution among the demobilizing soldiers of the French army. The Bolsheviks presumably expected that the vigilance of the Allies would relax with the advent of peace, and therefore they would be better able to smuggle propaganda, agents, brochures, and even bombs across the frontier into France. French authorities, Pageot argued, should therefore maintain their observation of revolutionaries at home and abroad even after the ending of hostilities: "The danger is real and must not be neglected."[19]

Both French and British intelligence discounted the danger of Bolshevism in Germany: "No sensible person is taken in by the device."[20] The Germans, they argued, were only attempting to frighten the Allies into making a more generous peace by raising the spectre of Bolshevism. Berlin, moreover, was even accused of giving aid to the Bolsheviks in Switzerland, and therein lay the real danger to the interests of the Entente.

At a meeting of the Foreign Ministers at the Quai d'Orsay on November 1, the French representative, Stephen Pichon, asserted that France had little to fear from the Bolsheviks, but the Italian, Baron Sidney Sonnino, insisted that Italy faced great danger. The main center of Bolshevik propaganda lay in Switzerland, he warned, and "the Allies ought to be much on their guard as to what was happening there."[21]

The British seem to have been the most aloof to the question of Bolshevism. On the one hand, the Foreign Office had been insisting all year that the Swiss authorities could handle the matter themselves when they chose to, and on the other, the British representatives in Bern had repeatedly insisted that they saw no immediate danger to England in these matters.[22] The Italians were the most anxious and the French the most forceful, but none of the diplomats seemed particularly well informed about Bolshevik activities. Whatever details Pageot could offer his colleagues, the diplomats repeatedly fell back to characterizing the developments as being under the direct command of Lenin and Trotsky. Now and again they spoke of Balabanova. The diplomats had no comprehension of the genuine appeal which the Bolshevik Revolution had for western radicals.

The Central Powers were also anxiously watching the events in Switzerland. Writing on November 4, the Austrian ambassador noted the growing fear of Bolshevism: "Bolshevism, many remember, came from Switzerland." The Bolshevik forces in Switzerland, he reported, "do not lack money. The country has become an exchange point for Bolshevik revolutionary ideas."[23]

On November 1 the Bundesrat met in secret to discuss the question of the growing threat of a general strike in the country. Its deliberations soon turned to the general activity of the Soviet mission. Expressing fear that Russian couriers were importing revolutionary literature and voicing concern about the amount of Russian money "deposited in Geneva and Zurich banks," the council agreed that it had enough grounds to act against the mission, which, it felt, was seeking to prepare and spread revolution. The Bundesrat directed the Political Department to investigate how to limit "the Russian agents and disturbers of the peace who come into Switzerland and under the cover of Russian couriers (such as Zalkind, Balabanova, etc.)."[24]

On November 2 Paravicini informed Shklovsky that Balabanova and Zalkind should leave Switzerland immediately. Shklovsky promised his response on Monday, the fourth, and when he returned, he declared that Balabanova could in fact leave immediately, but that Berzin would like to know the specific reasons for her expulsion. Zalkind, on the other hand, would first have to obtain a German visa. Paravicini reiterated that the two must leave immediately, although the Swiss hesitated to put this in the form of an ultimatum.[25]

According to Zurich police, Balabanova left their city for Bern on November 1; in her memoirs, Balabanova told of receiving a telegram in Zurich, summoning her to the Soviet mission, where she learned of the Swiss government's demand.[26] In contrast to Shklovsky's statement to Paravicini, she informed Berzin that she would "refuse to leave the country under such conditions unless the leaders of the Swiss labour unions decided that it was better for their movement that I should do so."[27] Apparently forgotten was her original resolve to remain only two weeks in Switzerland, as she appealed for, and received, the support of the Swiss Socialist Party and of labor union leaders.

Berzin took her case directly to Bundesrat Müller, bypassing Paravicini, and requested that Balabanova be permitted to remain another two weeks in order to complete her work for the Russian Red Cross. He essentially admitted Müller's complaint that she had as yet done nothing in this direction, but Müller in turn indicated that she might be granted this limited extension. Contradicting Shklovsky's statement to Paravicini, Berzin indicated that Zalkind was expendable; he could leave the country immediately.[28]

On the morning of November 4 the French minister, Paul Dutasta, just recently returned from Paris, complained to Calonder that the Swiss government was not acting firmly enough against the rising Bolshevik threat: "One is left with the impression that the authorities are too timid and fearful toward these people." The Bolsheviks had allegedly brought fifty million francs into Switzerland, they had held a conference on the Beatenberg, and they were working to spread revolution into the countries of the Entente. Why was Balabanova in Switzerland? "In the event that Bolshevism spread more in Switzerland, France would be compelled to close off the border with Switzerland by a cordon."

Calonder attempted to calm Dutasta, and he assured him that the Bundesrat was doing its duty but simply could not react to "all foolish rumors." Immediately after this meeting, however, Calonder went into a secret session with the Bundesrat to report on the demarche and to discuss the question "Bolsheviks in Switzerland."[29]

After hearing the president's report as well as an account of the Political Department's demand for the departure of Balabanova and Zalkind, Gustave Ador took the initiative in the Bundesrat's discussion, urging strong measures against the Soviet mission and calling for a press release denouncing foreign revolutionary activities in Switzerland. Müller objected that the Bundesrat still lacked hard facts; a press release at this time would be a mistake. The Justice Department was preparing a formal expulsion order, but it still lacked concrete evidence on cooperation between the Soviet mission and the radicals in Switzerland. (Müller at this point had not yet spoken with Berzin.) In the end, the Bundesrat chose to take no definite action, although it directed the Justice Department to prepare a public statement.[30]

Politicians, participants, and historians, discussing this sequence of events, have focused on a number of questions in attempting to explain the actions of the Bundesrat. Willi Gautschi, citing Dutasta's demarche, has indicated that he tended to agree with Robert Grimm's evaluation that the "stringpullers of the Entente" had arranged everything.[31] Balabanova asserted firmly that the "Allies and especially Italy" stood behind her expulsion. Lenin, in a letter of November 1 which Berzin probably did not receive, had warned his emissary that the Entente might force Switzerland to expel him: "Be ready!"[32]

Beyond the obvious question of Entente pressure lay the further consideration of the nature of this pressure. Many Swiss were convinced that the Entente was ready to invade Switzerland if the Bundesrat did not act firmly against the Bolsheviks. The evidence discussed above, however, suggests that at no time did the Allies actually discuss military intervention. Nor did Pageot give any serious consideration to this possibility in his many reports. This would indicate that the Allies had no such plans.

The fact that the Bundesrat had begun to act against Balabanova and Zalkind on November 1 would indicate that Dutasta's demarche was a contributing but not the decisive factor in the actions of the Swiss. Even Pageot's urgings and complaints would appear to have been more of an encouragement than a determinant. The formal demarches of the Entente diplomats began only after the Bundesrat had initiated its course of action. The ultimate initiative in the Bundesrat's decisions, therefore, would seem to have been its own perception of Swiss domestic affairs.

10: EXPULSION

Growing socialist unrest, compounded by the development of an influenza epidemic, the "Spanish grippe," brought heightened tension into Swiss public life in November 1918. The war between Germany and the Entente powers, which had seemed interminable, was now drawing quickly to its close, but already a new conflict tended to overshadow it, one between the Bolsheviks and the victorious Western powers. In the new conflict, as much ideological as physical, Switzerland could not maintain its neutrality; it had already become a battlefield. The western powers particularly feared Italy's vulnerability to revolutionary agitation, and Switzerland represented the invasion route.

On the evening of November 4, German railway workers in Berlin dropped one of twenty-three crates being unloaded as diplomatic pouch carried by a Soviet courier. From the broken crate spilled propaganda material which German authorities declared was aimed at arousing the German workers and soldiers to a bloody revolution. The next day the German Foreign Office ordered Joffe to leave the country immediately, and the German government broke off diplomatic relations with the Soviet regime.[1]

News of the incident in Berlin aroused new passions in Bern, as opponents of the Soviet mission argued that the diplomatic couriers had been carrying the same type of material to Berzin. Perhaps the intercepted crates had been in fact destined for Switzerland. (The Swiss government formally inquired on November 6.) In an open meeting on November 5, the Bundesrat ordered the Swiss border police to stop all Russians seeking entry

161

into the country and in each case to seek advice from the Fremdenpolizei: "Entrance is to be denied to Russians without papers, even escaped prisoners of war." The order, sent out through the Justice Department, reached the military only four days later. Another inquiry produced the information that no Russian couriers had entered the country since October 31.

In the absence of Calonder and Motta, the Bundesrat also met in a secret session on the fifth to continue their discussion of Balabanova's case. Müller reported having received a request by a delegation of Swiss Socialists to be allowed to speak on Balabanova's behalf, and he brought in Berzin's statement that Zalkind could leave the country immediately but that Balabanova really needed to stay another two weeks in order to complete her work for the Russian Red Cross. Although Müller claimed that Balabanova had had nothing to do with the Red Cross, he had told Berzin that this might be possible. Ador immediately objected that Balabanova should be deported as agreed, but Schulthess intervened to emphasize the need to avoid unnecessary trouble. The Bundesrat then decided, "Frau Balabanova's pass, which expires in fourteen days, should not be extended," in effect granting Berzin's wish.[2]

The delegation of Swiss Socialists, made up of Fritz Platten, Otto Lang, and Rosa Bloch, had given Müller a statement urging that Balabanova be permitted to remain. Her work with the Russian soldiers in Switzerland was of utmost importance, they argued. Moreover, "the international working class" had charged her, as international secretary, with the task of organizing a "conference of workers' representatives of all countries." Balabanova's expulsion, the statement warned, would be considered "an unfriendly act toward the Swiss Party and the whole Swiss organized working class." Such an act would bring forth "a general storm of indignation in the Swiss working class"; it would do nothing "to calm the aroused tempers of the working class."

A meeting on November 5 between Müller and Paravicini on the one hand and Platten, Lang, and Bloch on the other, drew together all the threads of tension in Swiss society. Against the background of mounting social unrest and turmoil, these Swiss citizens angrily debated the issues of the day as personified in Angelica Balabanova.[3]

Platten opened the meeting by informing Müller that the "leadership of the working class" accepted no responsibility for the consequences which might follow the deportation of Balabanova. Balabanova was the "secretary of the International and as such a person of greatest importance." She had come to Switzerland to prepare an international socialist conference—Platten did not mention the Red Cross or the interned Russian soldiers—and "this work cannot be disrupted by the Swiss government."

Müller responded that Paravicini had in fact not ordered Balabanova's expulsion but had rather requested her departure. Balabanova, he argued, had acted as an agitator in Switzerland, "a quality which, moreover, as already noted by Herr Platten, lies in her nature." In any case, her mission had formally concerned the work of the Russian Red Cross: "I hear now for the first time of a mission on behalf of international socialist arrangements."

Rosa Bloch took a motherly tone: "Frau Balabanova is a woman of great loving kindness. She is a true mother for all workers. Every worker would view her expulsion as a personal insult." Otto Lang attempted to minimize her possible revolutionary role: "Frau Balabanova is a significant woman, but the workers' movement does not depend on her presence. Whether she stays or must go, the question of the workers will not be influenced by that."

Paravicini interjected that Balabanova had ostensibly come to Switzerland to work for the Red Cross. By Shklovsky's own admission, she had done nothing in this regard up to now: "She shares hereby the fate of every person who comes to Switzerland on an official mission and does not concern himself with this mission."

Platten attempted to argue that Balabanova had not engaged in agitation but rather simply in discussions with Swiss comrades; he himself, however, then launched into revolutionary rhetoric: "Switzerland is the given country for an international enterprise such as Bolshevism. The movement is not to be stopped and will progress on its way despite such measures as the present expulsion order."

Paravicini and Müller stood firm against this onslaught. Müller declared that the Bundesrat would do what it had to in order to maintain public order; it would not allow itself to be influenced by threats. He admitted the existence of pressure from foreign governments in Balabanova's case, but he concluded the meeting by declaring that the Bundesrat would make its decision on Friday, November 8. Until then Balabanova could remain.

The Bundesrat met again on November 6 to hear Müller's report on his meeting with the socialists. Müller proposed still to take no further decisions on Balabanova: "The Jungburschen are only waiting for a favorable occasion to let loose." The Bundesrat generally agreed that there was now proof enough that the Soviet mission was attempting to use Switzerland as a revolutionary base, and Ador, the most outspoken partisan of the Entente in the group, insisted that all relations with the mission should be broken. He went on to propose a press release, declaring among other things that the Bundesrat will "act without weakness against all those foreign elements who participate in any way in the revolutionary or anarchist plots. It will not permit Switzerland to become a training ground for Bolshevik agitators." In the ensuing discussion, the other councillors expressed concern for the fate of Swiss in Russia, and Ador finally agreed to a postponement of such a press release, on the understanding that the Bundesrat had essentially decided to expel the Soviet mission. In a second session on the evening of the same day, the Bundesrat accepted Ador's press release; as part of its preparations for a move against the Soviet mission it also decided to make new requirements for identity papers, announced on November 5, retroactive.

Both the domestic and the external pressures on the Swiss government were now growing rapidly. On November 7, Calonder was shocked when Dutasta came to him to praise the Bundesrat's secret decision to act against the Soviet mission. The French minister went on to insist that the expulsion of the mission would of itself not suffice; the Swiss must also search the premises of the mission and of its agencies, seizing revolutionary literature and funds. Calonder explained that the Swiss were still considering the measures which they should take.

The English took no part in Dutasta's campaign, but they essentially endorsed his initiative. A Foreign Office official commented on the idea of expelling the Bolsheviks, "This drastic action on the part of the Swiss Government will be very welcome."[4] The Italians also took the occasion to warn the Swiss minister in Rome that they would not permit their neighbor to the north to become a "revolutionary source."[5]

The fate of the Soviet mission had now become

inextricably bound up with the rising social unrest in the country. Conservative sources were firmly convinced that the Olten "soviet" was drawing both inspiration and funding from the Russians. The *Gazette de Lausanne* of November 1 exclaimed, "It is truly stupifying that one has permitted a Bolshevik mission, whose obvious aim is to propagate—by iron and fire and by means of money plundered from banks—social progress as understood by Lenin, Trotsky, and their sinister band, to come in and install itself in full view in the federal capital." Rumors abounded concerning revolutionary plans.

The strike movement in Switzerland, with its threatening shadow of a general strike, grew apace. Zurich again served as the focus of the tension. The bank employees' strike of October had aroused considerable fear, and conservative circles spoke of a possible repetition which would bring a wholesale plundering of bank deposits. Some rich Swiss were reportedly even withdrawing their money. In the middle of October Zurich authorities notified President Calonder that troops would be necessary in their region; a general strike could break out at any time and this would lead to revolution. Zurich police could not contain the action, and the disturbances would undoubtedly spread throughout the country.[6]

On November 1 General Wille appeared before the Bundesrat to demand a mobilization of troops, but that body refused, arguing that major demonstrations were not planned for several days yet. Decoppet warned that a mobilization might in fact be considered a provocation, and his colleagues agreed that precipitate action might only increase the "danger of revolution." (The ever growing influenza epidemic also posed a threat to any mobilization.)

The next day, General Wille, who had already

drawn up his plans for mobilization, visited Zurich himself to examine the situation. He came away with disturbing impressions, not the least of which was advice to withdraw his money from the bank, and he summarized his feelings in a new memorial to the Bundesrat on November 4. Zurich faced, he declared, "the possibility of a sudden, unexpected outbreak of a revolution." The situation posed a threat to the "continued existence of the Swiss Federation." The task, as he saw it, was "to organize the counterrevolution which should recapture the cities which the revolution has taken away from us."[7]

Meeting with representatives from Zurich in an evening session on November 5, the Bundesrat agreed to call up two cavalry brigades and two infantry regiments as of 3 p.m. the next day. The troops were to be stationed in Zurich. On the evening of the sixth, in its third session of the day, the Bundesrat approved the mobilization of Switzerland's other two cavalry brigades and two more infantry regiments.[8]

November 7 marked the first anniversary of the Bolshevik seizure of power in Russia, and radicals throughout Switzerland planned demonstrations in honor of the occasion. On October 29 the Swiss Socialist Party had called for nationwide demonstrations; Fritz Platten distributed an outline for speeches to be given on the anniversary.[9] The conservative forces interpreted these preparations in their own way. The *Gazette de Lausanne*, which had taken a leading role in the anti-Soviet campaign, published a document purporting to be instructions to the Soviet mission concerning fostering strikes and planting "bon-bons" (bombs).[10] As *Der Bund* of November 7 saw it, "Switzerland, especially the great city of Zurich, should experience a putsch on the Bolshevik anniversary."

Zurich, however, was quiet on the seventh as the

newly mobilized troops marched through the city. Mass meetings were scheduled for Sunday the tenth. At the Soviet mission in Bern a festive dinner took place with Platten, Balabanova, and Guilbeaux all attending. The country generally saw no serious demonstrations. Backed now by the troops in place, the Bundesrat moved more firmly against the Soviet mission. On November 7 the Bundesanwaltschaft delivered its report on Balabanova. (Such reports were a necessary preliminary step for the Bundesrat to decide on expulsion.) Balabanova, it noted, had first appeared in Switzerland in 1902, and in 1906 had been excluded from the canton of Vaud for "anarchist propaganda." Recounting the various reports that Balabanova had brought money with her into Switzerland, the report failed to mention Platten's insistence that Balabanova's mission had been in fact to organize an international socialist conference. Summarizing instead some of her speeches and newspaper articles, the Bundesanwaltschaft recommended her expulsion.

In an open meeting on the seventh, the Bundesrat formally resolved that it had enough evidence to prove the revolutionary and anarchistic activities of the Soviet mission. Therefore it had decided to break off relations "with this mission which has never been formally recognized." The Bundesrat also endorsed a lengthy appeal to the Swiss people, the press release which Ador had demanded.

Addressed to "Loyal, dear countrymen," the Bundesrat's appeal spoke of the tribulations of neutrality and explained the decision to help the local authorities in Zurich: "Overtly or covertly certain groups and papers are threatening to transplant to Switzerland the revolutionary and anarchistic experiments which are cruelly afflicting Russia." Without mentioning the Soviet mission, the appeal emphasized that the Bundesrat's actions were aimed against no Swiss group, only against foreign influences.[11]

The Olten Aktionskomitee met in the evening of November 7 to consider the troop mobilization. At first ready to settle for just a protest declaration, the com- mittee then reconsidered the question and decided to call a twenty-four-hour protest strike in the nineteen larger industrial centers of the country for November 9. The strike apparently served two purposes: to express opposition to the mobilization, which the *Berner Tag- wacht* of November 8 denounced as a "provocation," and also to bring together under one roof all the ten- dencies within the socialist movement which were at this time threatening to break off and go their own ways.[12]

As the lines hardened between the government and its opposition, western diplomats repeatedly expressed satisfaction with the Bundesrat's decisions. Colonel Pageot had attributed the Bundesrat's weakness to an expectation that Germany would win the war; he now welcomed the Bundesrat's actions enthusiastically, crediting Dutasta with having given the Swiss moral courage: "This change of attitude is due in great part to the energetic action of His Excellency the Ambassa- dor."[13]

The strikes and demonstrations of Saturday No- vember 9 passed without incident. Zurich remained tense but quiet, as news began to reach Switzerland of revolutionary upheavals in Germany in the wake of its military defeat. On the morning of the tenth the Work- ers' Union of Zurich announced that it would continue the strike indefinitely until the government agreed to withdraw troops from the city, free all political prison- ers, reestablish the right to assembly, eschew penalties against the strikers, and recognize the Soviet mission. On the afternoon of the tenth a mass demonstration in the Fraumünsterplatz led to shooting in which three civilians were wounded and one soldier was killed. When the crowd attempted to reassemble in Milchbuckwiese to hear a speech by Platten, the cavalry attacked with drawn sabers.

Meeting in a special session on the tenth, the Bundesrat directed the Bundesanwaltschaft to order the Soviet mission out of the country by Monday night. On the evening of the tenth, the Olten Aktionskomitee, meeting in Bern, issued its own call for a general strike beginning at midnight November 11-12. The committee demanded a new election of the Nationalrat and listed a number of political and economic grievances; it made no mention of the Soviet mission in its declaration, although rumors spoke of secret demands for the resignation of General Wille and the members of the Bundesrat as well as for the annulment of the expulsion order against the Soviet mission.[14]

During all these developments, the Soviet mission kept its counsel. On November 8, when notified of the Bundesrat's decision to break relations, Berzin reportedly commented that "some members of his mission have probably lacked the necessary caution."[15] Faced by the Bundesrat's ultimatum of the tenth to leave Bern in barely more than twenty-four hours, Shklovsky won an extension of one day, agreeing to bring the members of the mission to the train station at 1 p.m. on Tuesday, November 12. (Some members of the mission had to be recalled from other parts of Switzerland.)

Individually, some members of the mission still maintained their personal activity in local radical circles. The Swiss authorities registered several complaints against Russians for delivering speeches in Bern on the evenings of the 10th and the 11th. Rumors circulated that the Bolsheviks had promised full pay to all the strikers and had given five million francs to the Olten Aktionskomitee.

One member of the mission, V. A. Miliutin, prepared a bitter attack on the Swiss government, "The Bundesrat Against Soviet Russia," for distribution by the Russische Nachrichten, but for some reason it was not published. When Swiss authorities discovered the manuscript a few days later, however, it was taken as evidence of the attitudes of the Soviet mission and used as ex post facto justification for the expulsion. Miliutin charged that the Swiss were attempting to imitate the Germans in forcing the Russians to leave the country. Out of fear of social revolution and also in an effort to win favor with the western powers, the Bundesrat had now demonstrated its "complete incompetence and short-sightedness." The Swiss workers will know what to do, the article concluded: "This government cannot and may not remain at its post. In imitating William [II of Germany] the Bundesrat is preparing its own fate."[16]

On the night of November 11-12, the Soviet mission hastily carried out its preparations for departure. At Shklovsky's direction, Dzerzhinskaia, who did not leave with the mission, burned "all the secret documents"; Fritz Platten, on November 8, had already taken six trunks and boxes from the building.[17] The mission entrusted the liquidation of its possessions to two Swiss lawyers: Franz Welti of Basel and Fritz Studer of Winterthur. Robert Grimm undertook the liquidation of the Russische Nachrichten.

On the morning of the twelfth, the Bundesrat completed its actions against the mission by formally ordering the expulsion of Balabanova and Zalkind. The members of the Soviet mission were both collectively and personally expelled from the country; Swiss authorities recorded the names with the intention of preventing any of the individuals involved from returning under any circumstances.

Determining the membership of the mission was

itself a formidable task since a number of diplomatic
couriers had entered the country and then broken off all
ties with the mission. Mark Natanson, for example, had
been publicly attacked as a major agent of revolution,
but he now requested permission to remain in the country for reasons of health. On the other hand, Steinberg
and Shreider both asked Berzin for permission to return
to Soviet Russia with the mission. Berzin agreed, declaring that the two men would have to stand trial in
Moscow for their participation in the revolt of the Left
Socialist Revolutionaries. The Swiss authorities drew no
such distinctions in their list of departing members of
the mission.

The travelers gathered at the mission on the
Schwanengasse at noon on Tuesday and proceeded to
make their way on foot to the train station. Since
Berzin was again ill, Shklovsky was in charge of all
arrangements. The call for a general strike, which had
met with a varied response in the country, had effectively closed all business activity in Bern. Large crowds
roamed through the streets of the city, and the Soviet
group met with both cheers and catcalls.

Balabanova was a special target of the onlookers.
As she later described the scene, "The eyes of all were
directed toward us, hands and canes were waving, mocking words sounded after us. The women were especially
active; their feeling of hatred and revenge made their
behavior irresistibly comic; they were hyenas, senseless
hyenas." When she heard whispers, "There she is, the
damned courier of revolution," Balabanova stepped out
of the group to confront the crowd. Disorders followed,
and she lost consciousness. When she awoke, the crowd
had withdrawn and her arm was bleeding. Soldiers accompanied her back to the group.[18]

At 2:30 the group was finally ready to travel. Since
the strike also prevented the trains from running, the

Swiss provided nine automobiles together with two trucks for luggage. Twenty-five Swiss soldiers were to accompany the group. When the lieutenant in charge informed the Russians that the soldiers had orders to shoot if anyone attempted to leave an automobile without permission, the representative of the Foreign Office, Thurnheer, had to intervene to calm Berzin down and to suggest that the lieutenant withdraw and remain quiet. Accompanied by dragoons, the caravan slowly made its way out of the city.[19]

The trip to the border at Kreuzlingen followed a route established by the Swiss General Staff. Only one of the automobiles was a sedan, seven had only cloth covers, and one was completely open. The weather was cold, and after a time it began to rain. Because of the bad roads, the trucks could not keep up with the cars and eventually had to follow another route for a time. The automobiles themselves, which had not been used for several months, gave trouble, and the caravan had been given only enough gasoline to reach Dietikon, near Zurich. When night came, it was discovered that some of the automobiles had no headlights.

At nine in the evening, the group stopped for food. The Swiss dared not halt in a town of any size which might have industrial workers, and therefore they chose an inn in a small village, Hunzenschwil, where the soldiers apparently received much better service than the foreigners did. At 10:30 the group set on its way again, but one truck and two automobiles had to be deserted on the road for lack of gasoline. Shklovsky, who had been riding in one of the abandoned automobiles, had to take his place now in a truck. When the second automobile stopped, six members of the mission, including Shreider, had to remain with it, guarded by several soldiers.

The remaining seven automobiles reached Dietikon

at one in the morning, where the refueling stop lasted about an hour. According to the report of the Foreign Office's representative, the most difficult part of the trip now followed in the third stage, from Dietikon to Unter-Embrach. Traveling in the dark on second class roads, the caravan had to make frequent stops in order to reassemble its membership. In one case, a wrong turn could be rectified only by a tortuous retracing of their path, at the cost of an hour in the frosty dawn: "This mishap seemed about to bring several men of the Soviet mission completely out of control." The Russians demanded breakfast in a city, and the column stopped in the next village, Unter-Embrach. The "entire village gathered" to see the visitors.

The fourth stage from Unter-Embrach to Kreuzlingen enjoyed better conditions: sunshine and good roads. Only one automobile had to be sent to Winterthur for minor repair. One baggage truck had trouble keeping the pace. At noon the column pulled into Emmishofen, near Kreuzlingen; the trip had taken twenty-one and a half hours, some fifteen on the road and six at various stops. Somehow, the automobile left behind on the road to Dietikon had already arrived in Kreuzlingen.

The Foreign Office's representative, Dr. Jacob, later reported that the members of the mission had generally behaved very well in the course of the journey. Only a few, especially Zalkind, "believed it necessary to give manifold evidence of their Russian temperament," denouncing the trip as a scandal, threatening to make the Swiss mission in Russia walk to the frontier, and so on. It must be admitted, Jacob noted, "that the trip was somewhat difficult as a result of its length and the palpable cold."

To the dismay of all concerned, the Swiss discovered at the border that they could not yet rid themselves of their guests. Although the government had requested permission of the revolutionary government of Bavaria for the Soviet mission to pass, the German border guards would not admit the group. The Swiss considered pushing the Russians across the border at some unguarded spot, but then decided to put them up for the time being at an inn in Emmishofen.

The Germans finally agreed to receive the Russians, but because of a shortage of trains, they asked the Swiss to keep them yet a while. The Germans did not consider it feasible to keep the Russians under guard in Konstanz; the Swiss could do the job more easily. When informed of this situation, members of the mission wanted to negotiate themselves with the German border guard, but the Swiss refused to permit them to leave their inn. Ten members of the mission, including all the women, received beds for the night; the rest slept on straw.[20]

At this point, one of the thirty-three travelers, P. E. Karklin, announced that he was in fact a Swiss citizen, having married a Swiss woman. The Swiss authorities refused to recognize his claims and forced him to remain with the group. Eventually the Germans separated him out and returned him to Switzerland.

The Germans had at first indicated their readiness to accept the Russians on the morning of the fourteenth, but on Thursday evening they announced that because of a delay in organizing a formal committee of reception, they could not admit the group until the fifteenth. The Russians therefore spent Friday making requests of their Swiss guards. Jacob agreed to send mail and telegrams concerning personal matters, but he refused permission to make telephone calls.

When Jacob came to collect the group for the crossing on the morning of the fifteenth, he was astounded to meet with new demands, presented by Shklovsky, that the travelers have formal documents guaranteeing them passage through Germany. Up to this point, the Russians had seemed only concerned with leaving Switzerland as soon as possible. With great effort, Jacob persuaded them to proceed without further conditions. Since the Swiss General Strike had now ended in what seemed to be a great victory for the Bundesrat, the group was able to board a train for the short ride to Konstanz.[21] They had no trouble in passing through Germany and even caught up with Joffe's group at the Russian frontier.

The western diplomatic community in Bern watched the Bundesrat's struggle with the strike and its actions against the Soviet mission generally with sympathy. They welcomed the end of the general strike but they felt that the revolutionary dangers were not yet over. The French urged the Swiss yet to expel the "hundreds of mysterious beings who, calling themselves socialist, very easily penetrate workers' circles." Although the general strike had failed, the agitators might yet renew their efforts "since they are for the most part unconscious agents of an inspiration which comes both from Russia and from Germany and which does not seem about to disarm."[22]

The diplomats also criticized the Swiss for their failure to seize the documents and archives of the Soviet mission. While hailing the Bundesrat's "crushing victory" over the Bolsheviks, Rumbold reported, "It has been suggested that the omission to search the luggage and papers of the mission was caused by the fear that documents of the most compromising nature to some Swiss national councillors would be found." Curiously, while Rumbold in one report called the expulsion of the Soviet mission long overdue, in another he spoke of it as a "somewhat illtimed though laudable decision."[23]

Rumbold's complaint about the archives of the mission was later to be repeated by several generations of Swiss historians. The federal commission set up to investigate the activity of the Soviet mission concluded that its task had been greatly hindered because the mission had "been permitted to take along all documents without any control. . . . Through this rule by which the Swiss observed international law, the important evidence was lost from the beginning for the investigation."[24]

In fact, the Swiss government acquired a great deal of information which its agents simply failed to evaluate. In a series of raids aimed at the associates of the mission who had been permitted to remain in Switzerland—including Maria Bratman, Bagotsky, Dvasia Shklovskaia, James Reich, and Ilia Milkich—the Swiss seized the archive of the Russische Nachrichten, containing the correspondence of Isaak Schweide, as well as a large volume of personal correspondence of the principals. They also collected considerable oral testimony.

The Russians yet in Switzerland served as hostages against the treatment of the Swiss in Soviet Russia, but the Swiss government found itself embarrassed in this matter by its own internal confusion. The Soviet government did not immediately permit Junod and Odier to leave Russia. On December 12, the Political Department ordered the Swiss frontier guard to treat Shklovskaia, Bratman, Liubarskaia, Bagotsky, and Wetsozol as hostages; they were not to be permitted to leave the country. The Bundesanwaltschaft, however, received no notification of this action, and on January 14, 1919, it directed Bern police to order Shklovskaia, Dzerzhinskaia, Bratman, Reich, and Milkich to be on trains leaving Basel on the sixteenth for both Poland and Russia. The Bern police accordingly informed the persons mentioned of their deportation.

The Swiss socialist press reported the deportation orders with renewed attacks on the Swiss authorities. The Basel *Vorwärts* of January 17 urged the Soviet government to take revenge against Odier and Junod for this "abominable treatment of women and children by the federal authorities, this filthy and mendacious policy." These cries grew in intensity when the Swiss frontier guard, acting under the orders of the Political Department, ordered Shklovskaia, Liubarskaia, and another woman off the train because of their status as hostages. (Guilbeaux was also taken off the train because of the refusal of German authorities to allow him passage; he successfully crossed the frontier a month later.)

The Soviet government now demanded the right to send a new delegation to Switzerland to clean up the affairs of the Berzin mission, but after some deliberation, the Bundesrat refused. In the spring, the two sides reached a compromise. The Swiss agreed to allow Shklovskaia and Liubarskaia to stay or to leave as they wished, and the Russians permitted the Swiss diplomats to return home. For the Swiss authorities, this posed several more complications. On the one hand, the Political Department had to prevail upon the Bundesanwaltschaft to drop its expulsion order against Shklovskaia and Liubarskaia, and on the other the Political Department found it difficult to persuade Shklovskaia's landlady to permit her to remain in her old residence.[25] Liubarskaia left the country in April 1919, but Shklovskaia departed only on September 28, 1920.

EPILOGUE

Swiss officials followed the expulsion of the Soviet mission with a variety of moves against radical elements in the country, deporting groups from virtually every major city. These included Ganchak, Schweide, and many Italians. The net was broadly cast, and many anti-Bolsheviks on the left found themselves deported as a consequence. This proved particularly upsetting for the Socialist Revolutionaries, but the Swiss authorities drew no fine distinctions. The government expelled Willi Münzenberg in November 1918, deciding that he no longer faced personal danger at the hands of the German revolutionary government. In 1919, after a variety of delays, the government expelled Guilbeaux, also through Germany.

All this effort won the Swiss little credit from the Entente. Woodrow Wilson had at first favored holding the Peace Conference in either Lausanne or Geneva, but on November 7 he criticized Switzerland as being "saturated with every poisonous element and open to every hostile influence in Europe." Undoubtedly influenced by the French desire to hold the conference in Paris and by the French criticism of Switzerland, the Americans expressed fear for the safety of peace delegates if the gathering should take place in Switzerland.[1]

In the succeeding years, relations between the Swiss and the Soviet governments remained virtually nonexistent. Sergei Bagotsky served as the unofficial Soviet representative. The assassination of V. V. Vorovsky in April 1923 by a White Russian emigré when the Soviet diplomat was in Switzerland to attend the Lausanne conference on the Straits brought more complica-

179

tions to this troubled relationship and only in 1946, in the aftermath of World War II, did the two states resume diplomatic relations.

The events of November 1918 cut deeply into the Swiss body politic, leaving wounds which were not to heal for generations, if at all. On the one side, conservative forces remained convinced that the Bolsheviks had been planning and inciting revolution, that Swiss radicals had acted as willing, eager tools of Moscow. The government's investigation, the so-called "Bolschewiki-Untersuchung," could prove nothing in this regard, but the legend lived on. As the years went by, it was even embellished with such ideas as the assertion that Karl Radek was to be the dictator of Bolshevik Switzerland.[2] On the other side, the Swiss left consistently argued that the domestic uproar was independent of the presence of the Soviet mission, and that the Bundesrat had either erred gravely or acted provocatively in associating the two so closely.[3] But the Swiss Socialist Party in turn always felt embarrassed, after it had turned against the Comintern, by the fact that Lenin had indeed played a major role in its development from 1914 to 1921.[4]

The evidence indicates that the Soviet mission had little interest in revolutionizing Switzerland just for its own sake. The directives from Moscow were at best vague, and the Bolshevik supporters in Switzerland were rather undependable. Even Fritz Platten, considered one of Lenin's most loyal followers, drew the Bolshevik leader's wrath: "They say that the Swiss atmosphere is having a bad influence on you (this atmosphere is too petty bourgeois, too 'peaceful', too 'comradely')."[5] Platten withdrew from the Olten Aktionskomitee in August, and that committee must be considered a domestic Swiss phenomenon, not an imported product.

Berzin's task called for the dissemination of revolutionary literature, of preparing the ground for revolution but not necessarily of carrying through a revolution.[6] All Bolsheviks who thought about it had to recognize that the Entente powers would not tolerate a Bolshevik Switzerland.

At the end of November 1918, Berzin, now in Moscow, gave his own evaluation of the mission's work, when he spoke to the Central Executive Committee of the Congress of Soviets. After first transmitting greetings from "the revolutionary proletariat of Switzerland," he recounted that the Swiss had admitted him only grudgingly: "We were admitted only on the condition that we would not conduct revolutionary propaganda. . . . But despite this we continued our work of revolutionary propaganda. Our expulsion testifies that we accomplished this work." His greatest diplomatic success, he asserted, came in the liquidation of the Onu legation.

More important, Berzin continued, was "our informational work." This involved both disseminating and collecting information. Since the mission was not to engage in open propaganda, "we did not appear at meetings, and we did not publish in newspapers under our own names." Nevertheless the mission managed to inform the workers of Switzerland and of other countries about events and conditions in Russia: "This was the real purpose of our representation in Switzerland."

Berzin identified the American minister in Bern, Pleasant Stovall, as the moving force in bringing about the Bolsheviks' expulsion, and he explained that Switzerland "represented an excellent observation post during the war. . . . This aspect of the work of our representation also had a rather great significance."[7] In addition, Berzin offered an interpretation of the Swiss General Strike which Soviet historians were hereafter to accept: "In this way the first general strike derived from solidarity with our October Revolution and from solidarity with our socialist policy."[8]

Berzin's account, reaffirmed by his article in *Prav-*

da in January 1925, emphasized the propaganda activities, and probably correctly, but the mission also played a role in the gradual development of a Third International. In a way, especially after Balabanova's coming, it represented an effort to organize cooperation among Western European radicals. Particularly striking is the number of members of the mission who took part in the founding of the Communist International in 1919. First Balabanova and subsequently Berzin acted as secretaries; in the 1920's Humbert-Droz became secretary. Guilbeaux represented France at the Comintern's founding congress, Milkich represented Serbia, and Platten Switzerland. Gorter and Dzerzhinskaia also took part in the meeting. Liubarsky later played an important role in the politics of the Italian Socialist Party, while James Reich first took over the publications of the newly formed Comintern and subsequently headed the Comintern's Secretariat for Western Europe.

One should not, however, overemphasize the degree of international organization which the Bolsheviks could realize in 1918. The shoots which would grow into the Communist International were still tender indeed; many could not survive. Guilbeaux, Gorter, and others were not to remain long in the Bolshevik camp, because while they could agree with the Leninist attitude toward the war, they were not ready to follow the lead of the Bolsheviks in the postwar world too. The ranks of Bolshevik sympathizers were in a constant flux in this period, and in historical retrospect some of the Bolsheviks' supporters in 1918 or even 1920 seem oddly out of place.

However much it inspired certain groups, the Bolshevik revolution remained essentially a Russian phenomenon; Trotsky's vision on the morrow of the revolution of a world without diplomatic codes and state secrets proved ephemeral. Revolutionary phrases could not bring down the capitalist order, and the Soviet government itself began to study the ways of co-existence with governments of differing social and economic systems, just as the western governments eventually had to reconcile themselves with the existence of the Soviet government in Russia. So long as the hope of revolution lingered, the Russians could view this co-existence as temporary; when eventually this hope waned in the 1920's, the Soviet leadership had to reconsider its views of the world. Revolution and diplomacy became more distinct activities, independent of each other.

The experience of the Berzin mission came at a time of renewed hope in revolution; the breathing space won by signing the Treaty of Brest-Litovsk with Imperial Germany seemed to be leading into a period of a new revolutionary wave sweeping through Europe. As emigrés before the revolution, many of the Bolshevik leaders had personally learned the advantages of working within the borders of a neutral state such as Switzerland.

In a way the Berzin mission therefore represented a picture of successful revolutionaries returning to the site of much of their training.[9] Switzerland had sheltered them in their time of flight; now they returned as victors, offering an example to others. The deeds and accomplishments of the Bolsheviks would have served to excite the ardent spirits of western radicals even had the Bolsheviks not considered this arousal a part of their program.

In this endeavor, the Bolsheviks drew heavily on lessons learned during the years of emigration. The use of a Swiss publishing house as a front for the dissemination of Lenin's writings found its antecedents in the old practice of using the names of Swiss citizens as the editors of emigré newspapers in order to shield the publications from any restrictions on the part of the Swiss government. The emigré colonies, moreover, which had provided anywhere from one-fourth to one-third of the total number of students at the seven universities of Switzerland before the war, provided a considerable pool of talent from which Berzin could draw.

The makeup of Berzin's mission eloquently testified to the Soviet government's image of itself. Having proclaimed the liberation of the minority nationalities of Imperial Russia as well as heralding the beginning of world revolution, the Bolsheviks recruited freely among radicals of all nationalities;[10] Europe had probably not seen such a cosmopolitan diplomatic service since the time of the French Revolution. In later years, the Soviet government limited itself more to its own citizenry in selecting diplomats.

Western diplomats generally could not comprehend the nature of the Berzin mission. Thinking in traditional terms of nations and states, they did not understand the Bolsheviks' call for class struggle and social revolution. Absorbed as they were in the struggle with Germany, the diplomats tended to see the Bolsheviks as little more than agents of Berlin. The international appeal of the Bolshevik revolution had no meaning for them.

In all, the Berzin mission must find its place in history as an embodiment of Lenin's conception of the necessity to "prepare for and wage a revolutionary war." At Brest-Litovsk the Bolsheviks had admitted the impossibility of waging a revolutionary war, but Lenin had not abandoned his aim to rouse "the socialist proletariat of Europe to insurrection against its governments and in spite of its social chauvinists." This did not yet mean revolution; it meant the preparation of revolution, the education of the proletariat. Such had been Berzin's task.

ABBREVIATIONS

AA	Bonn, Auswärtiges Amt. Politisches Archiv.
AAM	Bonn, Auswärtiges Amt, Politisches Archiv, Microfilm. Series/Roll/Frame.
BBAr LGS	Bern, Bundesarchiv. Landesgeneralstreik. Cited according to page of the Index.
Ber Brunner	*Bericht des Ersten Staatsanwaltes A. Brunner an den Regierungsrat des Kantons Zürich über die Strafuntersuchung wegen des Aufruhrs in Zürich im November 1917 (vom 9. November 1918).* Zurich, 1919.
DVP	*Dokumenty vneshnei politiki SSSR.* 17 vols. Moscow, 1959–
FMA	Ministère de la Guerre. Etat-Major de l'Armée. Archives Historiques. Campagne contre l'Allemagne (1914-1918). 2e Bureau. Attaché Militaire. Suisse.
MGStAr	Munich. Geheim Staatsarchiv.
NZZ	*Neue Zürcher Zeitung.* Zurich.
OAr	Okhrana Archive. Stanford University. Hoover Institution.
PRO, F.O.	Public Records Office, Foreign Office.
PSS	V. I. Lenin, *Polnoe sobranie sochinenii.* 5th edition. 55 vols. Moscow, 1960-64.
USFR	United States State Department. *Papers Relating to the Foreign Relations of the United States.* Washington, D.C.
USNA	United States National Archives. State Department Decimal File, 1910-1929.
VSAr	Vienna, Staatsarchiv.
Zimm. Bew.	Horst Lademacher, ed., *Die Zimmerwalder Bewegung.* 2 vols. The Hague, 1967.
ZStAr	Zurich, Staatsarchiv.

NOTES

NOTES TO INTRODUCTION

1. Julius Braunthal, *History of the International*, 2 vols. (London, 1967), 2:163.

2. Cf. the treatment of the I.S.C. in: E. H. Carr, *The Bolshevik Revolution 1917–1923*, 3 vols. (London, 1950–1953), 3:157–60; James Hulse, *The Forming of the Communist International* (Stanford, 1964), pp. 2–3; Jules Humbert-Droz, *Origines de l'Internationale Communiste* (Neuchâtel, 1968), pp. 215–33; Olga Hess Gankin and H. H. Fisher, *The Bolsheviks and the World War: The Origin of the Third International* (Stanford, 1940), pp. 683–704; Angelica Balabanoff, "Die Zimmerwalder Bewegung 1914–1919," *Archiv für die Geschichte des Sozialismus und der Arbeiterbewegung*, 13:258–84; N. E. Korol'ev, *Lenin i mezhdunarodnoe rabochee dvizhenie 1914–1918* (Moscow, 1968), pp. 229–89; Branko Lazitch and Milorad Drachkovitch, *Lenin and the Comintern*, vol. 1 (Stanford, 1972).

3. Cf. Richard H. Ullman, *Anglo-Soviet Relations 1917–1921*, 3 vols., (Princeton, 1961–72), 1:60–62, 78–81; A. U. Pope, *Maxim Litvinoff* (New York, 1943), pp. 128–38.

4. Cf. the rather unreliable account in G. A. Solomon, *Sredi krasnykh vozhdei* (Paris, 1930); Louis Fischer, *Men and Politics* (New York, 1966), p. 26; Winfried Baumgart, *Deutsche Ostpolitik 1918* (Vienna, 1966), pp. 334–63.

5. See Willi Gautschi, *Der Landesstreik 1918* (Zurich, 1968); Paul Schmid-Ammann, *Die Wahrheit über den Generalstreik von 1918. Seine Ursachen, Sein Verlauf, Seine Folgen* (Zurich, 1968); Leonhard Haas, *Carl Vital Moor. Ein Leben für Marx und Lenin* (Zurich, 1970).

6. L. I. Trofimova, "Pervye shagi sovetskoi diplomatii," *Novaia i Noveishaia Istoriia*, 1972, no. 1, pp. 68–72; Mikh. Sonkin, *Kliuchi ot bronirovannykh komnat* (Moscow, 1970), pp. 174, 216.

7. Cf. *Lenin v bor'be za revoliutsionnyi Internatsional* (Moscow, 1970), esp. pp. 397–400.

NOTES TO CHAPTER 1
Bolshevik Foreign Policy

1. *DVP*, 1:11–14. Cf. the variant interpretations of the decree in E. H. Carr, *The Bolshevik Revolution 1917-1923*, 3 vols. (London, 1950–1953), 3:9–19; George F. Kennan, *Russia Leaves the War* (Princeton, 1956), pp. 74–77, and also his *Russia and the West under Lenin and Stalin* (Boston, 1960), pp. 33–37; Adam B. Ulam, *Expansion and Coexistence* (New York, 1968), pp. 52–55; and S. Iu. Vygodskii, *Leninskii dekret o mire* (Leningrad, 1958).

2. *Izvestiia*, November 9, 1917.

3. L. D. Trotskii, *Sochineniia*, 21 vols. (Moscow, 1925–1927), 3(2):164–65: *DVP*, 1:21–22. See also M. P. Iroshnikov and A. O. Chubar'ian, *Tainoe stanovitsia iavnym* (Moscow, 1970).

4. *PSS*, 27:48–51, 282–93. Italics in the original. Lenin used the term "social chauvinist" to refer to Social Democrats who were supporting their government's war effort.

5. *PSS*, 32:287, 34:232–33.

6. Leon Trotsky, *My Life* (New York, 1930), p. 341. Trotsky objected to the quotation as a simplification, but he accepted its spirit. On the choice of the title "People's Commissar" instead of "Minister," see *ibid.*, pp. 337–38. Isaac Deutscher, *The Prophet Armed: Trotsky, 1879-1921* (London, 1954), p. 352, characterized Trotsky's work in the following way: "Even as Foreign Secretary he remained the revolution's chief agitator. He started almost everything on the potential or actual antagonism between the rulers and the ruled."

7. *DVP*, 1:14–15, 34–35.

8. Jacques Sadoul, *Notes sur la révolution bolchevique* (Paris, 1971), p. 216; Louise Bryant, *Six Red Months in Russia* (New York, 1918), pp. 200–201. See also Zalkind's memoirs, "NKID v semnadtsatom godu," *Mezhdunarodnaia zhizn'*, 1927, no. 10, pp. 12–20; A. Startsev, *Russkie bloknoty Dzhona Rida* (Moscow, 1968), p. 183.

9. For a recent Soviet account of these events, see A. O. Chubar'ian, *V. I. Lenin i formirovanie sovetskoi vneshnei politiki* (Moscow, 1972), pp. 65–66.

10. For accounts of the negotiations, see John W. Wheeler Bennett, *The Forgotten Peace: Brest-Litovsk, 1918* (New York, 1939); Trotsky, *My Life*, pp. 362–78.

11. *DVP*, 1:67–70.

12. Angelica Balabanoff, *My Life as a Rebel* (London, 1938), p. 183. On the history of the Zimmerwald movement and

of Lenin's Zimmerwald Left, see Horst Lademacher, ed., *Die Zimmerwalder Bewegung*, 2 vols. (The Hague, 1967); Olga Hess Gankin and H. H. Fisher, *The Bolsheviks and the World War* (Stanford, 1940); Alfred Erich Senn, *The Russian Revolution in Switzerland, 1914–1917* (Madison, Wis., 1971).

13. Cited in L. I. Trofimova, "Pervye shagi sovetskoi diplomatii," *Novaia i noveishaia istoriia*, 1971, no. 6, p. 43. Chubar'ian, *Lenin i formirovanie sovetskoi vneshnei politiki*, p. 71, quoted Vorovsky's charge as "to inform the whole foreign world about the revolution in Russia."

14. V. D. Bonch-Bruevich, *Na slavnom postu. Pamiati V. V. Vorovskogo* (Moscow, 1923), p. 1. See also Vorovsky's memoir in his *Sochineniia*, 3 vols. (Moscow, 1933), 3:358–64, and his *Stat'i i materialy po voprosam vneshnei politiki* (Moscow, 1959), pp. 179–85; G. A. Solomon, *Sredi krasnykh vozhdei* (Paris, 1930), pp. 11–12; Balabanoff, *My Life*, pp. 199–200, and also her *Erinnerungen und Erlebnisse* (Berlin, 1927), pp. 181–83; Ia. Ganetskii, *V. V. Vorovskii. Biograficheskii ocherk* (Moscow, 1925), pp. 53–57.

15. Balabanoff, *My Life*, p. 200.

16. *Ibid.*, p. 183.

17. See *Pravda*, December 26, 1917; M. I. Trush, *Vneshnepoliticheskaia deiatel'nost' V. I. Lenina 1917–1920 den' za dnem* (Moscow, 1963), pp. 77–78; M. P. Iroshnikov, "Iz istorii organizatsii Narodnogo Komissariata Inostrannykh Del," *Istoriia SSSR*, 1964, no. 1, p. 115. On December 27, the Bolsheviks declared banking a state monopoly in Russia and ordered the existing banks to transfer their assets and liabilities to the State Bank.

18. Balabanoff, *Impressions of Lenin* (Ann Arbor, 1964), p. 29.

19. See *Lenin v bor'be za revoliutsionnyi Internatsional* (Moscow, 1970), pp. 397–98.

20. On the problem of arranging for Holzmann's visit to London, see George Buchanan, *My Mission to Russia and Other Diplomatic Memories*, 2 vols. (Boston, 1923), 2:241–43.

21. *PSS*, 35:243–52.

22. R. H. Bruce Lockhart, *Memoirs of a Russian Agent* (London, 1932), p. 224; Kennan, *Russia Leaves the War*, pp. 401–5, 429.

23. *PSS*, 35:391.

24. Cf. the argumentation in Ia. M. Sverdlov, *Izbrannye proizvedeniia*, 3 vols. (Moscow, 1959), 2:135–40.

25. *Izvestiia*, February 7, 1918. In January 1918 Chicherin

told a British diplomat that the Bolsheviks "are now busily engaged in organising a new International in which there would be no room for moderate socialists like [Karl] Branting and [Arthur] Henderson." Lockhart, *Memoirs of a British Agent*, p. 222.

26. Sverdlov, *Izbrannye proizvedeniia*, 2:112–14; *Lenin v bor'be za revoliutsionnyi Internatsional*, pp. 398–400; Francis to Secretary of State, Feb. 19, 1918, USNA, 861.00/1150.

27. Balabanoff, *Impressions of Lenin*, p. 29.

28. "Mezhdunarodnaia revoliutsiia i neitral'nye strany," *Izvestiia*, January 27, 1918.

NOTES TO CHAPTER 2
Swiss Neutrality

1. Text of the exchange between Hoffmann and Grimm in Olga Hess Gankin and H. H. Fisher, *The Bolsheviks and the World War* (Stanford, 1940), pp. 621–22. The concierge of the Swiss mission reportedly delivered the text to the French socialist Albert Thomas. See Paul Schmid-Ammann, *Die Wahrheit über den Generalstreik von 1918* (Zurich, 1968), pp. 78–79. See also *Zimm. Bew.*, 1:575–644; the report of the Russian minister in Bern, July 19, 1917, reprinted in *Izvestiia*, January 7, 1918; Paul Stauffer, *Die Affäre Hoffmann/Grimm* (Zurich, 1973).

2. British report dated April 17, 1916, PRO, FO 371/2766A/77354; minute to a report from Bern, FO 371/2766A/63810; Okhrana report no. 753, July 20/August 2, 1916, OAr, VIIIb, f. 11. On the intelligence activities of the warring powers, see Walter Nicolai, *Geheime Mächte. Internationale Spionage und ihre Bekämpfung im Weltkrieg und heute* (Leipzig, 1924), translated as *The German Secret Service* (London, 1924); Clemens von Walzel, *Kundschaftsdienst oder Spionage?* (Vienna, 1934); L. Lakaz, *Chetyre goda razvedyvatel'noi raboty 1914–1918* (Moscow, 1937).

3. Sir Horace Rumbold to London, January 31, 1918, PRO, FO 371/3379A/24711; intelligence report in files of FMA.

4. Stovall to Secretary of State, December 10, 1917, USNA, 861.00/787; Romberg to Berlin, September 9, 1918, AAM, T149/146/00043; report of Adolf Müller, March 21, 1918, MGStAr, MA I (Polit Arch), no. 951.

5. *NZZ*, no. 1292, September 9, 1914. See also Edgar

Bonjour, *Swiss Neutrality: Its History and Meaning* (London, 1946).

6. Cf. Hartmut Lehmann, "Die Haltung Österreich-Ungarns zum Nationalitätenproblem der Schweiz im ersten Weltkrieg," *Historische Zeitschrift*, 198:575–613.

7. Report dated October 27, 1917, FMA.

8. See Z. V. Gempp, *Geheimer Nachrichtendienst und Spionageabwehr des Heeres* (Berlin, 1940).

9. PRO, F.O. 371/3379A/193352.

10. Charles Lucieto, "In a German Den at Berne," in *Modern Spies Tell Their Stories*, Richard R. Rowan, ed. (New York, 1934), p. 5.

11. Leonhard Haas, *Carl Vital Moor. Ein Leben für Marx und Lenin* (Zurich, 1970), p. 179; *NZZ*, nos. 202, 214, 231, February 10, 12, and 16, 1918.

12. *Recueil de documents secrets tirés des archives de l'ancien Ministère des Affaires Etrangères Russe* (Geneva, 1917), pp. 33–46. Upon first delving into the work of the Tsarist foreign service, Svatikov had characterized the situation in Switzerland as a "cesspool." Svatikov to N. A. Rubakin, September 5, 1917. Rubakin archive, Lenin Library, Moscow, 273/24.

13. *USFR, 1918 Russia*, 3 vols. (Washington, D.C., 1931), 1:549.

14. On the formation of the Russian Political Conference in Western Europe see John M. Thompson, *Russia, Bolshevism, and the Versailles Peace* (Princeton, 1966), pp. 66–78. On the work of Tsarist diplomats in Switzerland before the revolutions of 1917, see V. N. Firstova, "Tsarskaia diplomaticheskaia missiia v Berne i russkaia emigratsiia," *Voprosy istorii*, 1973, no. 6, pp. 205–207.

15. See Willi Gautschi, *Der Landesstreik 1918* (Zurich, 1968), pp. 71–79; Heinz Egger, *Die Entstehung der Kommunistischen Partei der Schweiz* (Zurich, 1952), pp. 96–100; W. Bretscher and E. Steinmann, *Die sozialistische Bewegung in der Schweiz 1848–1920* (Bern, 1923), pp. 96–108.

16. Bretscher and Steinmann, *Die sozialistische Bewegung*, pp. 93–94.

17. *PSS*, 30:196–208, 31:87–94.

18. See O. V. Sventsitskaia, "Priezd Fritsa Plattena k V. I. Leninu v Petrograd," *Novaia i noveishaia istoriia*, 1972, no. 2, pp. 66–75. Curiously Platten received a visa from the British to travel with Zalkind and Kamenev, but he did not use it.

19. A British report of November 1918 spoke of Nobs as

being Platten's "lieutenant" and described him as "an unpleasant person and a devotee of Bolshevism." PRO, F.O. 371/3317/1917. Cf. Nobs's own account, "Lenin und die Schweizer Sozialdemokraten," *Rote Revue,* 33:49–64. On Lenin's relations with the Swiss Socialists, see Alfred Erich Senn, *The Russian Revolution in Switzerland, 1914–1917* (Madison, Wis., 1971), pp. 204–18.

20. Willi Münzenberg, *Die dritte Front* (Berlin, 1929), pp. 69, 75.

21. Ferdi Böhny, "Die sozialistische Jugendbewegung des Ersten Weltkrieges als politischer Faktor," *VPOD. Der öffentliche Dienst* (reprint, 1964).

22. Münzenberg, *Die dritte Front,* p. 184.

23. *Ber. Brunner,* pp. 70–71; police reports of April 30, 1917, and March 4, 1918, in ZStAr, P239.14.

24. Fritz Brupbacher, *60 Jahre Ketzer. Selbstbiographie* (Zurich, 1935), p. 191; Münzenberg's deposition to Zurich police, March 27, 1918, ZStAr, P239.14. See also Egger, *Die Entstehung der KPS,* p. 52.

25. Markus Bolliger, *Die Basler Arbeiterbewegung im Zeitalter des Ersten Weltkrieges und der Spaltung der Sozialdemokratischen Partei* (Basel, 1970), p. 70; Münzenberg, *Die dritte Front,* p. 232.

26. See the conflicting reports in *Volksrecht,* January 16, 1918, and in the Zurich police report, January 17, 1918, ZStAr, P239.14.

27. On Misiano see Franco Pieroni Bartolotti, *Francesco Misiano. Vita di un internazionalista* (Rome, 1972); John M. Cammett, *Antonio Gramsci and the Origins of Italian Communism* (Stanford, 1967), pp. 143–52.

28. BBAr, LGS, S. 310. See also Helmut König, *Lenin und der italienische Sozialismus 1915–1921* (Tubingen, 1967), p. 20.

29. See Balabanova's letters to Guilbeaux, undated, BBAr, LGS, S. 304–5; also Annie Kriegel, *Aux origines du communisme français 1914–1920* (Paris, 1964), pp. 197–202.

30. Jules Humbert-Droz, *Mon évolution du tolstoïsme au communisme, 1891–1921* (Neuchâtel, 1968), pp. 234–78. Also based on an interview with M. Humbert-Droz, May 5, 1970, in La Chaux-de-Fonds.

31. See Edgar Bonjour, *Swiss Neutrality,* p. 128; *NZZ,* no. 1622, December 6, 1914, and nos. 5 and 121, January 1 and 24, 1916.

32. Intelligence report of November 1918, PRO, F.O. 371/3377/1917; minute to Rumbold's report of February 5,

1918, concerning Italian anarchists in Switzerland, 371/3377/ 1917; Rumbold to London, November 15, 1918, 371/3317/ 25416.

33. See Gautschi, *Der Landesstreik*, pp. 86–94; Gautschi, *Dokumente zum Landesstreik 1918* (Zurich, 1971), pp. 64–76.

34. Report of October 13, 1918, FMA.

NOTES TO CHAPTER 3
The First Emissaries

1. Bern to Petrograd, December 20, 1917, and Petrograd to Bern, December 24, 1917,BBAr, LGS, S. 251.

2. Memorandum of Albert Picot to the Political Department, January 23, 1918, BBAr, LGS, S. 251.

3. See Hans Töndury, "Russlandschweizer und Russen in der Schweiz," *Schweizerische Zeitschrift für Volkswirtschaft, Betriebswirtschaft und Sozialpolitik*, 34:167–78.

4. BBAr, LGS, S. 251.

5. Cf. George F. Kennan, *Russia Leaves the War* (Princeton, 1956), p. 83.

6. K. D. Nabokov, *Ispytaniia diplomata* (Stockholm, 1921), pp. 190–93; S. Iu Vygodskii, *U istokov sovetskoi diplomatii* (Moscow, 1965), pp. 45–48.

7. The Foreign Office records of the reception of Litvinov are to be found in PRO, F.O. 371/3298/1869.

8. Lockhart met Litvinov before his departure and received a personal introduction to Trotsky. R. H. Bruce Lockhart, *Memoirs of a British Agent* (London, 1932), pp. 201–4; Richard H. Ullman, *Anglo-Soviet Relations*, 3 vols. (Princeton, 1965–72), 1:60–62, 78–81.

9. G. V. Chicherin, *Stat'i i rechi* (Moscow, 1961), p. 53.

10. Karpinsky's announcement in *NZZ*, no. 33, January 7, 1918. Upon the announcement of Karpinsky's appointment, some Swiss sources charged him with complicity in the notorious Bolshevik bank robberies in Tiflis in 1907. See *Journal de Genève*, January 9, 1918. Once back in Russia, Karpinsky turned to propaganda work. See his *Mir ili voina* (Petrograd, 1918).

11. *NZZ*, no. 242, February 18, 1918.

12. See his interviews in *La Sentinelle*, February 13, 1918, and *Volksrecht*, March 16 and 18, 1918.

13. Unless otherwise noted, the following account is based

on reports to be found in BBAr, LGS, S. 250. Cf. the erroneous account in L. I. Trofimova, "Pervye shagi sovetskoi diplomatii," *Novaia i noveishaia istoriia,* 1972, no. 1, p. 65.

14. See Henri Guilbeaux, *Du Kremlin au Cherche-Midi* (Paris, 1933), p. 166.

15. Police report, February 19, 1918, ZStAr, P239.14.

16. See O. V. Sventsitskaia, "Priezd Fritsa Plattena k V. I. Leninu v Petrograd," *Novaia i noveishaia istoriia,* 1972, no. 2, pp. 66–75; A. Ivanov, *Frits Platten* (Moscow, 1963), p. 58.

17. BBAr, LGS, S. 250.

18. Horwitz and his wife received a bad report from their neighbors: "They receive very many visits from foreign revolutionaries, mostly Russian and Polish, and they argue into all hours of the night." Police report, February 23, 1918, BBAr, LGS, S. 250.

19. The leader of the student group was Maximilian Rivosh, whom Zurich police characterized as the revolutionary son of respectable parents: " . . . his parents idolize him and do not see what all he does behind their backs." Report of February 23, 1918, BBAr, LGS, S. 250.

20. On July 19, 1918, Platten presented the Soviet mission in Bern with a bill for 43.80 francs to cover the expenses of this trip, which he declared was taken "on orders from Lenin and Chicherin." BBAr, LGS, S. 366.

21. See Rumbold's account of a conversation with Calonder, March 2, 1918, PRO, F.O. 371/3377/1917.

22. Bern police report, February 28, 1918, BBAr, LGS, S. 250.

23. ZStAr, P239.14.

24. Willi Münzenberg, *Die dritte Front* (Berlin, 1929), p. 252.

25. I. Zal'kind, "NKID v 1917-om godu," *Mezhdunarodnaia Zhizn',* 1927, no. 10, p. 20.

26. "X," "Une mission en Occident," *Demain,* 26:90. Unless otherwise noted, the following account of Zalkind's voyage is based on this article which he himself wrote.

27. Note that Nabokov, *Ispytaniia diplomata,* p. 180, complained that the British let them in without first checking with the French. See also Ullman, *Anglo-Soviet Relations,* 1:81. Zalkind had to go through Scandinavia because as a Russian citizen, he could not yet travel through Germany. His wife was living at this time in Paris; she later joined him in Switzerland.

28. BBAr, LGS, S. 251.

29. Litvinov note, February 26, 1918, PRO, F.O. 371/3298/1869.
30. Report of the Political Department, March 5, 1918, BBAr, LGS, S. 250.
31. See "X," "Une mission," *Demain*, 26:90–95; "L'aventure de Kameneff et Zalkind," *Demain*, 24:417–19; Henri Guilbeaux, *Du Kremlin*, pp. 169–70.
32. French intelligence report in PRO, F.O. 371/3317/25415; Zal'kind, "NKID," *Mezhdunarodnaia Zhizn'*, 1927, no. 10, p. 20; Kennan, *Russia Leaves the War*, pp. 401–5; Balabanova to Guilbeaux, undated letter, BBAr, LGS, S. 305 (letter listed as written by unknown author).
33. Guilbeaux, *Du Kremlin*, pp. 168–70.
34. Pageot's report dated May 18, 1918, FMA; Rumbold's report, September 28, 1918, PRO, F.O. 371/3317/25416. *La Nouvelle Internationale* of May 11, 1918, listed an anonymous donation of 1000 francs "pour le triomphe des idées internationales."

NOTES TO CHAPTER 4
The Struggle for Recognition

1. On Joffe's own conception of his work in Berlin, see Louis Fischer, *Men and Politics* (New York, 1966), pp. 26–27.
2. See Berzin's *Partiia bol'shevikov v bor'be za kommunisticheskii internatsional* (Moscow, 1931), S. Ziemelis, *Janis Berzinš-Ziemelis. Dzives un darba apskats* (Riga, 1971), esp. pp. 178–86.
3. Instruction of April 23, 1918, BBAr, LGS, S. 251.
4. See Leonhard Haas, *Carl Vital Moor. Ein Leben für Marx und Lenin* (Zurich, 1970).
5. Mercier to Bern, April 26, 1918, BBAr, LGS, S. 251.
6. BBAr, LGS, S. 251.
7. Mercier to Bern, May 10 and 11, 1918, BBAr, LGS, S. 251.
8. See Mercier to Bern, May 14, 1918, BBAr, LGS, S. 251; Noske to Nadolny, May 14, 1918, AAM, T149/146/00668.
9. Bern to Berlin, May 14, 1918, and Mercier to Bern, May 15, 1918, BBAr, LGS, S. 251.
10. See Petrograd to Bern, May 23, 1918, Bern to Petrograd, June 1, 1918, BBAr, LGS, S. 251; Litvinov to Foreign Office, June 7, 1918, PRO, F.O. 371/3298/1869.

11. Swiss military reports, May 16 and 18, 1918, BBAr, LGS, S. 251; *Leninskii Sbornik*, 37:72, 76.

12. L. I. Trofimova, "Pervye shagi sovetskoi diplomatii," *Novaia i noveishaia istoriia*, 1972, no. 1, p. 70; *NZZ*, no. 689, May 27, 1918; Bern to Petrograd, June 1, 1918, BBAr, LGS, S. 251.

13. Rumbold to London, May 29, 1918, PRO, F.O. 371/3298/1869.

14. Egger to Bern, June 3, 1918. The Swiss maintained only a consul in Stockholm, subordinated to the mission in Berlin.

15. Calonder, as President and head of the Political Department, was formally in charge of Swiss foreign relations. The Foreign Office, a division of the Department, was headed by Charles Paravicini with Thurnheer as his deputy. Paravicini had once been secretary of the Swiss mission in St. Petersburg.

16. Correspondence in BBAr, LGS, S. 251. Viz. a blank page for Russia in *Schweizerischer Staatskalender 1918* (Bern, 1918), pp. 87–88.

17. *Agence de presse russe Bern*, May 22, 1918; *Berner Tagwacht*, May 21, 1918.

18. Rumbold to London, May 29, 1918, PRO, F.O. 371/3298/1869.

19. See *Der Bund*, May 31, 1918. The Bolsheviks claimed never to have seen the police. The report in the *Berner Tagwacht*, May 31, 1918, to the effect that Onu had yielded without a struggle was completely false.

20. BBAr, LGS, S. 254.

21. *Ibid.*

22. See Paravicini's letter to Calonder, May 28, 1918, BBAr, LGS, S. 254.

23. Political Department memorandum, May 29, 1918, BBAr, LGS, S. 254.

24. Rumbold to London, May 29, 1918, PRO, F.O. 371/3298/1869. The packets, still in the British archives, were of no political significance. According to the American minister: "Confidentially it is stated that important archives were put in place of safety three months ago." *USFR, 1918 Russia*, 3 vols. (Washington D.C., 1931), 1:548–49.

25. Memorandum by Paravicini, May 30, 1918, BBAr, LGS, S. 254.

26. Political Department memorandum, May 30, 1918, BBAr, LGS, S. 254.

27. Rumbold to London, May 31, 1918, and June 3, 1918, PRO, F.O. 371/3298/1869.

28. Protocol of sequestration, May 30, 1918, BBAr, LGS, S. 254.

29. Memorandum, May 31, 1918, BBAr, LGS, S. 254.

30. Golovan to Paravicini, June 20 and 24, 1918, and Paravicini to Golovan, June 22, 1918, BBAr, LGS, S. 254. Golovan then turned to the French for help, and Pageot reported to Paris that the Russian had "always taken a very correct attitude." Pageot to Paris, August 29, 1918, FMA.

31. See *Der Bund,* May 31, 1918, and *Basler Nachrichten,* June 2, 1918.

32. BBAr, LGS, S. 254.

33. PRO, F. O. 371/3298/1869.

34. Memorandum by Paravicini, June 21, 1918, BBAr, LGS, S. 253; See also *La Suisse,* June 23, 1918.

35. *DVP SSSR,* 1:467–68.

36. Mercier to Bern, June 14, 1918, BBAr, LGS, S. 253.

37. Mercier to Bern, June 24, 1918, BBAr, LGS, S. 253.

38. Telegrams in BBAr, LGS, S. 253.

39. *PSS,* 50:102.

40. At the beginning of 1918 the Swiss had generally tightened their regulations on foreign couriers of all countries. See PRO, F.O. 371/3379A/18230.

41. Bern to Mercier, June 26 and 27, 1918, BBAr, LGS, S. 253.

42. Bern to Mercier, June 27 and July 5, 1918, Mercier to Bern, June 28, 1918. See also the exchanges between Suter and Lev Karakhan in Moscow, described in Suter's dispatches of June 29 and 30, September 17, 1918. BBAr, LGS, S. 253.

43. G. V. Chicherin, *Stat'i i rechi* (Moscow, 1961), p. 57.

44. BBAr, LGS, S. 253.

NOTES TO CHAPTER 5
Diplomacy and Paradiplomacy

1. Rumbold to London, June 1 and 3, 1918 PRO, F.O. 371/3298/1869; Pleasant A. Stovall, *Switzerland and the World War* (Savannah, 1939) p. 230.

2. Stovall to Secretary of State, August 22, 1918, USNA, 861.00/2558.

3. Musulin to Vienna, September 6, 1918, VSAr, PA XXVII, Bd. 62.

4. *NZZ*, no. 58, January 12, 1918.

5. See *Agence de presse russe*, June 29 and July 3, 1918; Stovall to Secretary of State, June 6, 1918, USNA, 861.00/2149.

6. See the reports in PRO, F.O. 371/3328/89626; Skrzynski's report, January 29, 1918, VSAr, PA XXVII, Bd. 61.

7. See the inquiry of the British consul in Geneva, July 18, 1918, and the Foreign Office's response, August 10, 1918. PRO, F.O. 371/3328/89626. The Austrian ambassador questioned whether the League was not a violation of Swiss neutrality. Musulin to Vienna, July 15, 1918, VSAr, PA XXVII, Bd. 62. On American contacts with the anti-communist emigrés in Switzerland, see George F. Kennan, *The Decision to Intervene* (Princeton, 1958) pp. 430–31; Mitchell Price Briggs, *George D. Herron and the European Settlement* (Stanford, 1932), pp. 135–49.

8. Rivosh to J. Dailis, September 22, 1918, BBAr, LGS, S. 370–71.

9. Rivosh to N. A. Rubakin, n.d., Rubakin Archive, Lenin Library, Moscow, 267/35.

10. Report of Lausanne police, November 8, 1918, BBAr, LGS, S.306. On November 9 Pageot characterized Ganchak as violent, insolent, and unscrupulous. FMA.

11. See I. Ia. Solov'ev, *Vospominaniia diplomata* (Moscow 1963), pp. 326–36; AAB, Ges. Bern, Russland II. Sonderheft über Personen, Bd. I. British sources reported that Soloviev had alienated Entente diplomats in Madrid by publicly declaring his support of the deposed Tsar. Report from Madrid, March 6, 1918 PRO, F.O. 371/3298/1869. See also A. Nekludoff, *Diplomatic Reminiscences* (London, 1920), pp. 520–21.

12. The most complete available account of Moor's life is Leonhard Haas, *Carl Vital Moor. Ein Leben fur Marx und Lenin* (Zurich, 1970). See also H. Schurer, "Karl Moor—German Agent and Friend of Lenin," *Journal of Contemporary History*, 1970, no. 2, pp. 131–52; and C. E. Schuddekopf, "Deutschland zwischen Ost und West. Karl Moor und die deutsch-russischen Beziehungen in der ersten Hälfte des Jahres 1919," *Archiv für Sozialgeschichte*, 1963, no. 3, pp. 223–63.

13. Haas, *Moor*, p. 156.

14. See Leonhard Haas, *Lenin. Unbekannte Briefe 1912–1914* (Zurich, 1967).

15. *PSS*, 49: 447.

16. Haas, *Moor*, pp. 185, 192–94.

17. *Ibid.*, pp. 196, 206–13.
18. BBAr, LGS, S. 285; Willi Münzenberg *Die dritte Front* (Berlin, 1931), p. 255.
19. *Tribune de Lausanne,* August 11, 1918; *Berner Tagwacht,* August 13, 1918; *Der Bund,* August 13, 1918.
20. French report, September 23, 1918, weekly report, August 17, 1918, FMA; Haas, *Moor,* pp. 214–20.
21. Haas, *Moor,* pp. 220–24; *Der Bund,* September 2, 1918.
22. See *Der Bund,* August 21, 1918.
23. Reports of August 20 and September 4, 1918, FMA.
24. Romberg to Berlin, September 9, 1918, AAM, T149/146/00043.
25. *DVP, SSSR,* 1:472–75; *USFR, Russia 1918,* 3 vols. (Washington, D.C., 1931), 1: 697–98. 705–8.
26. Rumbold to London, September 28, 1918, PRO, F.O. 371/3377/1917.
27. Published separately by Volksrecht as *Ein diplomatischer Notenwechsel über den weissen und roten Terror,* September 30, 1918.

NOTES TO CHAPTER 6
Personalities and Assignments

1. Reports of the observation, BBAr, LGS, S. 253; Rumbold to London, September 28, 1918, PRO, F.O. 371/3317/25416.
2. Musulin to Vienna, September 6, 1918, VSAr, PA XXVII, Bd. 62; Willi Gautschi, *Der Landesstreik 1918* (Zurich, 1968), p. 162.
3. Gautschi, *Der Landesstreik,* p. 16.
4. Rumbold to London, July 5, 1918, PRO, F.O. 371/3299/1869.
5. *PSS,* 50:194, 201; Ia. Berzin, "Iz vospominanii o V. I. Lenine," *Pravda,* January 21, 1925. For some reason, possibly just an oversight, Lenin's letter of October 18, published by Berzin in *Pravda,* does not appear in *PSS,* 50.
6. His doctoral dissertation was entitled *Beitrag zur Kenntnis der Banda-Macis* (Bern, 1917), 30 pages. Shklovsky's wife Sarah received an M.D. in 1910 for her dissertation *Beziehung der retroversio uteri zu Gravidität und Geburt* (Bern, 1910), 27 pages.

7. BBAr, LGS, S. 284.

8. See BBAr, LGS, S. 284; *Bundesblatt der schweizerischen Eidgenossenschaft*, 1921, 2:383.

9. In all, Shklovsky's records seem to have been tidier than those of the mission in Berlin, which allegedly distrusted German banks. See G. A. Solomon, *Sredi krasnykh vozhdei* (Paris, 1930), pp. 59–61.

10. In mid-June Platten and Zalkind sought to travel to France, but the French government refused to grant them visas. PRO, F.O. 371/3317/26574.

11. On Gorter, see Helmut Gruber, *International Communism in the Era of Lenin* (New York, 1967), pp. 219–20, 231–40; Frits Kool, ed., *Die Linke gegen die Parteiherrschaft* (Olten, 1970), pp. 80–92.

12. See *NZZ*, no. 162, January 14, 1967.

13. S. Dzerzhinskaia, *V gody velikikh boev* (Moscow, 1964), pp. 269–70; N. Zubov, *F. E. Dzerzhinskii, biografiia* (Moscow, 1971), pp. 219–21; R. H. Bruce Lockhart, *Memoirs of a British Agent* (London, 1932), pp. 257, 326–36; report of the British consul in Lugano, November 22, 1918, PRO, F.O. 371/3377/1917.

14. Report of July 29, 1918, BBAr, LGS, S. 286.

15. Pageot's assertion that the Swiss had found arms in Rembelinsky's apartment when they raided it in November was false. Pageot's report, November 20, 1918, FMA; BBAr, LGS, S. 306.

16. BBAr, LGS, S. 286.

17. The mission gave 300 francs to each needy Russian adult making the trip in October, 200 francs for each child aged 6 to 16, and 100 francs for each child under 6. The group which left in October included civilians.

18. See Bagotsky's deposition, July 21, 1919, BBAr, LGS, S. 286; *Polozhenie russkikh voennoplennykh i deiatel'nost' komissii Rossiiskogo Krasnogo Kresta v Shveitsarii* (Bumplitz, 1918); Viktorov-Todorov's memorandum, November 9, 1918, PRO, F.O. 371/3317/25416; "Russische Kriegsflüchtige in der Schweiz," *Der Bund*, November 6, 1918.

19. See Leonard Schapiro, *The Origin of the Communist Autocracy* (New York, 1965), pp. 116–25; Lockhart, *Memoirs*, pp. 294–300.

20. According to the records of the Swiss consul in Moscow, he had granted Natanson a visa on May 14 and Steinberg his on May 30. The departure of two such well-known revolution-

aries was duly noted by western observers, who thought they were heading for Italy in order to engage in revolutionary activity there. A British diplomat added the melodramatic news: "They will travel through Germany and are being followed by two Czechs who will try to kill them." Petrograd to London, June 8, 1918, PRO, F.O. 371/3317/25416. Steinberg had served as the official translator for Fritz Platten's speech to the Third Congress of Soviets in January 1918.

21. Consul's reports, June 27 and 29, 1918, BBAr, LGS, S. 273.

22. *La Sentinelle*, October 1, 1918. Graber cited Shreider as his authority on the policies of the Left Socialist Revolutionaries. See also Romain Rolland, *Journal des années de guerre 1914–1919* (Paris, 1952), pp. 1625–26.

23. Correspondence in BBAr, LGS, S. 282.

24. Cf. Ellansky's analysis of the policies of the Left Socialist Revolutionaries in *Der Bund* of July 28, 1918. Ellansky was also a member, as a Latvian representative, of the Comité d'Est, organized by Edmond Privat and dedicated to studying the national question in Eastern Europe.

25. BBAr, LGS, S. 276; Rumbold to London, July 5, 1918, PRO, F.O. 371/3300/1869.

26. *PSS*, 50:201; *Pravda*, January 21, 1925.

27. See *PSS*, 49:343, 547.

NOTES TO CHAPTER 7
Information and Propaganda

1. *Pravda*, January 21, 1925. The press section was also a sizeable and important part of the Soviet mission in Berlin. See G. A. Solomon, *Sredi krasnykh vozhdei* (Paris, 1930), pp. 53–54.

2. *PSS*, 50:135, 193.

3. *PSS*, 50:194, 200, 201.

4. *PSS*, 50:182–84. Kautsky's article appeared in *Sozialistische Auslandspolitik*, no. 34 (August 1918).

5. *PSS*, 50:202; 37:101–10, 235–338.

6. This account of the founding of Russische Nachrichten and of Reich's career is based on Reich's testimony to Swiss officials, December 7, 13, and 18, 1918, BBAr, LGS, S. 285. On Reich's later career, see Branko Lazitch and Milorad Drachkovitch, *Lenin and the Comintern* (Stanford, 1972).

7. Reich's draft in BBAr, LGS, S. 285.
8. See Petropavlovsky's statement to Swiss officials, January 15, 1919, BBAr, LGS, S. 281.
9. BBAr, LGS, S. 285.
10. See Jordi's testimony, February 27, 1919, BBAr, LGS, S. 285.
11. Jacques Sadoul, *Notes sur la Révolution bolchevique. Octobre 1917—Juillet 1918*, Fritz Platten, ed. (Zurich, 1918); Henri Guilbeaux, *Du Kremlin au Cherche-Midi* (Paris, 1933), pp. 181–82.
12. Records of Russische Nachrichten, BBAr, LGS, S. 285.
13. See his memoir *Grazhdanin mira* (Moscow, 1930).
14. Peluso's correspondence in BBAr, LGS, S. 285.
15. Peluso's deposition to Swiss authorities, December 5, 1918, BBAr, LGS, S. 308.
16. See Alfred Erich Senn, *The Russian Revolution in Switzerland* (Madison, 1971), p. 148; Jerry H. Hoffman, "V. Stepankovsky, Ukrainian Nationalist and German Agent," *Slavonic and East European Review*, 50 (121):594–602.
17. BBAr, LGS, S. 376.
18. The British mission indirectly paid Peluso a compliment by noting, "Lenin and his agents appear to know the people on whom they can rely in Great Britain." Memorandum of November 2, 1918, PRO, F.O. 371/3317/25416.
19. This may have been the former Italian prisoner of war mentioned by Lenin in his letter to Berzin on August 3, 1918. *PSS*, 50:135.
20. Schweide's letters in BBAr, LGS, S. 285.
21. BBAr, LGS, S. 281.
22. BBAr, LGS, S. 276.
23. Kaclerovič's letter of January 12, 1918, and Nobs's of June 12, 1918, in BBAr, LGS, S. 278.
24. BBAr, LGS, S. 278. See also Iu. A. Pisarev, "Velikaia Oktiabr'skaia Revoliutsiia v Rossii i iugoslavianskie narody Avstro-Vengrii," *Etudes Balkaniques*, 1973, no. 1, p. 27.
25. Cf. L. I. Trofimova, "Pervye shagi sovetskoi diplomatii," *Novaia i noveishaia istoriia*, 1972, no. 1, p. 72, who interpreted the work of the mission as being mainly information and evaluated its accomplishments positively.

NOTES TO CHAPTER 8
The Guilbeaux Affair

1. Henri Guilbeaux, *Mon crime. Contre-attaque et offensive* (Geneva, 1918), p. 24.
2. As an example of the different ways in which the western governments perceived the activities of the Bolsheviks, one finds very little mention of Guilbeaux in the British and American archives, although for the French and the Swiss, who in this regard reflected the French influence, Guilbeaux played a major role in the work of the Soviet mission.
3. Guilbeaux, *Mon crime*, p. 22. See also his *Du Kremlin au Cherche-Midi* (Paris, 1933), p. 162, and Rosa Berzina's sympathetic comments, *Izvestiia*, July 20, 1918.
4. Guilbeaux, *Du Kremlin*, p. 171.
5. Lenin's letter, unpublished in *PSS* but reproduced in *Leninskii sbornik*, 37:86, is in BBAr, LGS, S. 304–5.
6. Pageot report, June 18, 1918, FMA. See also Annie Kriegel, *Aux origines du communisme français 1914–1920* (Paris, 1964), 1:200n.
7. Depositions by Schlesinger and Rosenberg in BBAr, LGS, S. 304–5.
8. English report, July 22, 1918, PRO, F.O. 371/3328/ 89626; *Zimm. Bew.*, 2:702.
9. Guilbeaux, *Du Kremlin*, pp. 162–63.
10. BBAr, LGS, S. 250.
11. BBAr, LGS, S. 304–5.
12. *Ibid.*
13. The Soviet mission had requested Dicker to enter the case. The Swiss Socialist Party also sent Guilbeaux a lawyer, Nationalrat Fritz Studer of Winterthur. See Guilbeaux, *Du Kremlin*, p. 176; Romain Rolland, *Journal des années de guerre 1914–1919* (Paris, 1952), pp. 1529, 1544–45, 1562–63.
14. Antrag of the Bundesanwaltschaft, August 21, 1918, BBAr, LGS, S. 304–5.
15. BBAr, LGS, S. 304–5.
16. See *La Sentinelle*, July 29 and August 5, 1918; Jules Humbert-Droz, *Mon évolution du tolstoïsme au communisme, 1891–1921* (Neuchâtel, 1969), pp. 277–78.
17. In his memoirs, Guilbeaux complained most about his isolation in prison. See his *Du Kremlin*, pp. 175–77.
18. Letter from Gorter to Guilbeaux, August 2, 1918, BBAr, LGS, S. 304.

19. Report of September 11, 1918, FMA.
20. Report of August 27, 1918, FMA.
21. See Guilbeaux, *Du Kremlin,* p. 177.
22. *Ibid.*
23. Reports of September 8, 10, and 17, 1918, FMA.
24. Guilbeaux, *Du Kremlin,* pp. 179–80. On September 2, Platten sent Lenin a letter recalling the assassination attempt of January and advising the Bolshevik leader to stay away from public gatherings. BBAr, LGS, S. 366.
25. BBAr, LGS, S. 304–5.
26. BBAr, LGS, S. 304–5. The precedent for this decision was the action of the Swiss government in limiting the activity of the Italian revolutionary Guisseppe Mazzini in 1869. See *NZZ,* nos. 1293 and 1301, October 2 and 3, 1918.
27. Guilbeaux, *Du Kremlin,* p. 187.
28. See *La Sentinelle,* October 8, 1918, Guilbeaux, *Du Kremlin,* p. 184.
29. Letter of October 15, *PSS,* 50:192. Italics in original.
30. See W. Bretscher and E. Steinmann, *Die sozialistische Bewegung in der Schweiz, 1848–1920* (Bern, 1923), pp. 128–30; Heinz Egger, *Die Entstehung der Kommunistischen Partei der Schweiz* (Zurich, 1952), p. 141; Willi Gautschi, *Der Landesstreik 1918* (Zurich, 1968), pp. 225–27.
31. *PSS,* 50:194, 199–200.
32. *Pravda,* January 25, 1925; Guilbeaux, *Du Kremlin,* p. 190. On the controversy between Guilbeaux and Balabanova, see below, chapter IX.
33. Report of October 30, 1918, FMA.
34. In reporting Humbert-Droz's meeting with Berzin Pageot indicated that the newspaper was to be "of clearly Bolshevik tendencies." In essentially confirming this story, Humbert-Droz told me that the newspaper was to defend the Soviet cause but not to be an official organ. Interview, May 5, 1970; Pageot's report, October 30, 1918, FMA.

NOTES TO CHAPTER 9
The Spectre of Revolution

1. See Pageot to Paris, October 30, 1918, FMA; Lord Acton to London, October 28, 1918, and Rumbold to London, November 15, 1918, PRO, F.O. 371/3317/25416 and 3377/1917.

2. Reports of October 27 and November 3, 1918, FMA.
3. BBAr, LGS, S. 266.
4. Telegram, Stockholm to Berlin, n.d.; Berlin to Bern,
July 29, 1918, BBAr, LGS, S. 266.
5. Letter to Berlin, July 29, 1918, BBAr, LGS, S. 266.
6. Telegram, July 30, 1918, BBAr, LGS, S. 266.
7. The Political Department to Fremdenpolizei, August 2,
1918; telegram, Bern to Berlin, August 3, 1918; Fremdenpolizei
to Stockholm, n.d.; Stockholm's acknowledgement, August 6,
1918. BBAr, LGS, S. 266.
8. Pageot's reports of September 17, October 16, 1918,
FMA; *Berner Tagwacht*, August 28 and September 14, 1918; Olga
Hess Gankin and H. H. Fisher, *The Bolsheviks and the World War*
(Stanford, 1960), pp. 686–87, 700–3.
9. See her *Erinnerungen und Erlebnisse* (Berlin, 1927), p.
190; *My Life as a Rebel* (London, 1938), pp. 209–10; *Impressions of Lenin* (Ann Arbor, 1964), p. 104; "Die Zimmerwalder
Bewegung," *Archiv für Geschichte des Sozialismus und der Arbeiterbewegung*, 13:283.
10. Balabanoff, *My Life*, pp. 210–13.
11. See *La Suisse*, October 26, 1918; Pageot's report of
November 7, 1918, FMA.
12. See Pageot's report of October 31, 1918, FMA.
13. Report of November 7, 1918, FMA.
14. See Guilbeaux, *Du Kremlin au Cherche-Midi* (Paris,
1933), pp. 172, 189; Balabanova's letters to Guilbeaux, BBAr,
LGS, S. 304–5.
15. In *Impressions of Lenin*, p. 104, she wrote of having
learned of the affair while in Stockholm; in *My Life*, pp. 214–15,
she indicated that the Italians in Zurich had first told her of it
when she arrived in Switzerland.
16. Among those coming up to talk with her was my
father, Alfred Senn, then a student at the University of Fribourg.
17. BBAr, LGS, S. 266.
18. Acton to London, November 5, 1918; report of British
consul, Lugano, November 22, 1918, PRO, F.O. 371/3377/1917.
19. See Pageot's reports of October 23, 30, and 31, 1918,
FMA.
20. Acton to London, October 28, 1918, PRO,F.O. 371/
3377/1917.
21. PRO, F.O. 371/3445/182649.
22. In a rather extreme example, in May and June the
British refused to become excited about a French report that the
Bolsheviks were smuggling communications into the Entente

6. Willi Gautschi, *Der Landesstreik 1918* (Zurich, 1968), p. 199.
7. Gautschi, *Dokumente*, p. 167.
8. Gautschi, *Der Landesstreik*, pp. 199–201.
9. Gautschi, *Dokumente*, pp. 155–57.
10. The British Foreign Office commented on this report, "The *Gazette de Lausanne* is given to publishing rather unreliable news and opinions on Slav subjects." PRO, F.O. 371/3377/1917.
11. See *Bericht des Bundesrates an die eidgenössischen Räte betreffend das Truppenaufgebot und die Streikunruhen* (Bern, 1918), pp. 2–4; *Der Bund*, November 9, 1918.
12. Gautschi, *Der Landesstreik*, pp. 248–49.
13. Pageot's report of November 8, 1918, FMA.
14. See Pageot's report, November 11, 1918, FMA.
15. Unsigned memorandum, probably by Paravicini, BBAr, LGS, S. 259.
16. Text in Gautschi, *Dokumente*, pp. 210–12.
17. Sofiia Dzerzhinskaia, *V gody velikikh boev* (Moscow, 1964), p. 273. Platten apparently feared for his own vulnerable position, and he turned the archives over to Otto Lang for safekeeping. They seem to have been subsequently lost.
18. Angelica Balabanoff, *Erinnerungen und Erlebnisse* (Berlin, 1927), pp. 196–97; *My Life as a Rebel* (London, 1938), pp. 217–18.
19. Gautschi, *Der Landesstreik*, p. 220; Gautschi, *Dokumente*, pp. 342–46.
20. Balabanova later insisted that she chose the straw. Jacob laconically reported, "As I later learned, various women preferred to spend the night in the straw in order not to feel too lonesome."
21. Jacob's report, Bern, November 20, 1918, BBAr, LGS, S. 261; Gautschi, *Dokumente*, pp. 347–62.
22. Reports of November 16 and 24, 1918, FMA.
23. PRO, F.O. 371/3377/1917 and 3317/25416.
24. *Bundesblatt der schweizerischen Eidgenossenschaft 1921*, 2:381–89. Cf. Edgar Bonjour, *Geschichte der schweizerischen Neutralität* (Basel, 1965), 2:694–95; Gautschi, *Der Landesstreik*, p. 224.
25. The landlady, a Frau Kümmerly-Frey, complained that after the expulsion of the mission, Shklovskaia's apartment had become the center of Bolshevik activities in Bern, and that this had upset the whole household. The Swiss government urged restraint on her, pointing to the uncertain fate of the some 1500 Swiss still in Soviet Russia. BBAr, LGS, S. 265.

NOTES TO EPILOGUE

1. See *USFR, Paris Peace Conference 1919*, 13 vols. (Washington, D.C., 1942–47), 1:119–20, 157. By way of contrast to the American interpretation of the choice of a site for the conference, see H. W. V. Temperley, *A History of the Peace Conference*, 6 vols. (London, 1920), 1:241–42.

2. Cf. *Les troubles révolutionnaires en Suisse de 1916 à 1919* (Lausanne, 1927), p. 40.

3. Cf. Paul Schmid-Ammann, *Die Wahrheit über den Generalstreik von 1918* (Zurich, 1968).

4. See Heinz Egger, *Die Entstehung der Kommunistischen Partei der Schweiz* (Zurich, 1952); Maurice Pianzola, *Le Parti Socialiste et l'ombre de Lenine* (Paris, 1954).

5. Letter from Lenin to Platten, August 14, 1918, *Leninskii Sbornik*, 37:99.

6. Cf. Willi Gautschi, *Der Landesstreik 1918* (Zurich, 1968), p. 157.

7. In September Berzin had told the Austrian minister that he saw the Americans as his major opponents, but the Swiss archives indicate that the French, in particular Col. Pageot, were the Bolshevik mission's most industrious antagonists. American intelligence sources seemed regularly slower than the French. See Leonhard Haas, "Der Landesstreik und das Ausland," *NZZ*, no. 654, October 23, 1968.

8. *Izvestiia*, November 17, 1918. See also Sofiia Dzerzhinskaia, *V gody velikikh boev* (Moscow, 1964), p. 272; Veridicus, *Suisse et Soviets, Histoire d'un conflict* (Paris, 1926).

9. For an example of the friendly feelings with which the Bolsheviks remembered Switzerland in 1918, see V. M. Velichkina, *Shveitsariia* (Moscow, 1918). Velichkina, the wife of V. D. Bonch-Bruevich, wrote (p. 240): "Diligently working and sincerely helping one another, the Swiss have achieved an order and well-being for which other larger states are still only striving. Little Switzerland is going on ahead of all of them."

10. The Soviet Constitution of July 1918, Part II, Chapter V, Article 20, provided: "Recognizing the solidarity of the workers of all nations, the Russian Socialist Federal Soviet Republic extends all political rights enjoyed by Russian citizens to foreigners working within the territory of the Russian Republic, provided that they belong to the working class or to the peasantry working without hired labour. It authorizes the local Soviets to confer upon such foreigners, without any annoying formalities,

the rights of Russian citizenship." *Materials for the Study of the Soviet System*, James H. Meisel and Edward S. Kozera, eds. (Ann Arbor, 1953), p. 81. This provision was dropped in the Constitution of 1936.

NOTE ON SOURCES

This study has been based first of all on the holdings of the Swiss Bundesarchiv in Bern. These include documents emanating from the Swiss Political Department as well as materials taken from individuals in the investigations which followed the expulsion of the Soviet mission. Particularly useful was the archive of the agency Russische Nachrichten. Since the agency had no formal tie with the mission, its archive was not covered by diplomatic immunity.

The Bundesarchiv brought these materials together as part of a project to study the history of the Landesgeneralstreik of November 1918. Since the collection was only temporary, I have cited the bound index in order to facilitate tracing the materials at a later time.

Of the other governmental sources, the archives of the French Ministry of War in Vincennes, containing the reports of the French military attaché Colonel Pageot, were particularly informative. The materials held by the Public Record Office in London are interesting but less significant. The French military attaché was obviously the Entente official most intensely involved in watching revolutionary developments in Switzerland.

The published documents of both the Soviet and the American governments (*Dokumenty vneshnei politiki SSSR*, vol. I, Moscow, 1959; and *Papers Relating to the Foreign Relations of the United States: Russia 1918*, 3 vols., Washington, D.C., 1932, and *Paris Peace Conference*, vol. 1, Washington, D.C., 1942) are of only limited value. The Soviet government seems to possess little documentary evidence concerning the work of the mission in Bern, and the American diplomats in Bern apparently understood little of the mission's activities. The archives of the German Foreign Ministry in Bonn and of the Austrian Foreign Ministry in Vienna contain interesting and valuable reports. At the same time, however, examination of these documents reveals nothing to support the claims of Entente diplomats and even of some historians that the Bolsheviks cooperated closely with the representatives of the Central Powers in Bern.

Turning to the published documents of the revolutionary movements of 1917-18, I found the collection *Die Zimmerwalder Bewegung*, Horst Lademacher, ed., 2 vols. (The Hague, 1967), indispensable in studying the history of the I.S.C. The interested student should also consult Olga Hess Gankin and H. H. Fisher, *The Bolsheviks and the World War* (Stanford, 1940); and Angelica Balabanova (Balabanoff), "Die Zimmerwalder Bewegung," *Archiv für die Geschichte des Sozialismus und der Arbeiterbewegung*, vol. 13 (1928), pp. 232-84.

Lenin's *Polnoe sobranie sochinenii*, 55 vols. (Moscow, 1960-64) is of course invaluable for such a study. Berzin's memoir first published in *Pravda*, January 25, 1925, has been reprinted a number of times in various collections of reminiscences about Lenin. I have already discussed in chapter nine the problems of using Balabanova's various memoirs. One should also consult Henri Guilbeaux's *Du Kremlin au Cherche-Midi* (Paris, 1935); Jules Humbert-Droz, *Mon évolution de tolstoianisme au communisme* (Neuchâtel, 1969); and Sofiia Dzerzhinskaia, *V gody velikikh boev* (Moscow, 1964). Useful biographies are: Leonhard Haas, *Carl Vital Moor. Ein Leben für Marx und Lenin* (Zurich, 1970); A. Ivanov, *Fritz Platten* (Moscow, 1963); and S. Ziemelis, *Janis Berziņš-Ziemelis. Dzīves un darba apskats.* (Riga, 1971).

For general background, besides the works mentioned in the Introduction, the reader might consult I. Zalkind, "NKID v semnadtsatom godu," *Mezhdunarodnaia zhizn'*, 1927, no. 10, pp. 12-20; Alfred Erich Senn, *The Russian Revolution in Switzerland* (Madison, 1971).

INDEX

A

Acton (Lord), 147
Ador, Gustave (1845-1928),
  25, 66, 158-59, 162, 164-65
Agence de presse russe, 29, 65,
  80
Ahre, Johann, 64
Akke, Artur, 64
Aktionskomitee (Olten), 38-
  40, 169, 170, 180
anarchists, 27, 31-34, 36
Arnold, Emil, 35
asylum, right of, 33-35, 38,
  129-30, 139-40
Avanesov, V. A. (1884-1930),
  100

B

Bagotsky, Sergei (1879-   ),
  101-5, 177, 179
Bahne, Ernst, 64
Bakherakht, V. R., 27-28
Balabanova, Angelica (1878-
  1965), Russian and Italian
  socialist, 14-15, 20-22, 24,
  36, 86, 134, 182; communications with Switzerland
  from Stockholm, 22, 35,
  37, 48, 55-56, 121; relations
  with Guilbeaux, 55-56, 110,
  129, 143, 150, 151, 154;
  travels to Switzerland, 148-
  52; activities in Switzerland,
  152-60, 162-64, 168; expulsion, 168, 171-72
Berlin, Soviet mission in, 1,
  3-4, 5, 59, 161
Bern, French mission in, 26-27
Bern, German mission in, 27
Bern, Imperial Russian mission
  in, 27-29, 65-73
Berner Tagwacht, 66, 137,
  140-41, 152, 169
Bertoni, Luigi, 137
Berzin, Jan A. (1881-1941),
  Soviet minister in Switzerland, 1, 5, 21, 57, 95, 108,
  118, 131-32, 135, 162, 172;
  named minister to Switzerland, 59-70, 87; relations
  with Joffe, 76-78; activity
  in Switzerland, 79-80, 83,
  96, 99, 104, 120, 157; attitudes toward other mem-
  bers of mission, 109-10,
  137, 142-43; instructions,
  111-13, 180-81, 184
Berzina, Rosa, 64, 125, 139
Bibikov, M. M., 28, 81
Biriukov, P. I., 37
Bismarck, Herbert von, 27
Bloch, Rosa, 162
Bratman, Maria (1888-   ),
  50, 82, 177
Bratman, Stefan (1880-1938),
  49, 50, 56, 81-82, 90, 98,
  103

Brest-Litovsk, peace negotiations at, 12-13, 16, 17-19, 41; treaty of, 19-20, 54, 59, 106, 130, 183
Brupbacher, Fritz (1874-1938), 31, 34
Bucher, Alfred, 35
Bund, Der, 109, 116, 140, 167
Bundesrat, Swiss Federal Council, 25, 33, 34, 38, 40, 63, 65, 70, 73, 91, 129-30, 139-40, 141, 144, 147, 157-60, 161-62, 164-65, 166-69, 171, 176, 178

C

Calonder, Felix Ludwig (1863-), 25-26, 64, 68, 77, 80, 93-94, 96, 158, 162, 165, 166
Cambon, Paul, 54
Chapiro, Joseph, 107
Charasch, Abram, 109
Chicherin, G. V. (1872-1936), Soviet Commissar of Foreign Affairs, 17-18, 45, 77, 92-94
Clemenceau, Georges (1841-1929), 26, 129, 130, 131
Comintern (Communist International), 2-3, 182

D

Declaration of the Rights of the Peoples of Russia, 11
Decoppet, Camille (1862-), 25, 166

Decree on Peace, November 8, 1917, 6-8
Demain, 37, 45, 48, 118, 130, 131, 133, 134, 138, 144
Dicker, Jacques (1879-1942), 48, 135, 137
Dickmann, Enrique, 122
diplomacy, Bolshevik views on, 4, 5, 6-11, 182-83
Divilkovsky, Anatole, 48-49, 50, 136-37
Dutasta, Paul, 26, 68, 129, 158-60, 165, 169
Dzerzhinskaia, Sofia (1882-), 50, 100-101, 171, 182
Dzerzhinsky, F. E. (1877-1926), 92, 100-101

E

Egger, Karl, Counselor of Swiss legation, Berlin, 61, 63, 75-76
Eisner, Kurt, 122
Ekke, Ernst, 64
Ellansky, Wladimir (Klavin), 108-9

F

Forderung, 34
Forel, Auguste, 137

G

Ganchak, Morduch, 82, 179
Gazette de Lausanne, 166-67
general strike, 4, 39, 157, 166, 169-72, 176, 181

Geneva, radicals in, 16, 48-49, 150
Golovan, S. A., 29, 69
Gornostaev, Leon A., 29, 73
Gorter, Herman (1864-1927), Dutch poet and radical, 99, 137-38, 182
Graber, Ernst Paul (1875-1956), Swiss socialist, 108, 137, 141, 142-44
Greulich, Herman (1842-1925), 32
Grimm, Robert (1881-1958), 14, 23-24, 39, 86, 87, 95, 130, 137, 140-41, 142, 151, 159, 171
Grimm, Rosa, 35, 61, 134
Grumbach, Solomon, 139
Guilbeaux, Henri (1885-1938), French radical, 36-37, 45, 81, 83, 99, 129-45, 178, 182; relations with Holzmann, 48, 50-51, 125, 130; relations with Balabanova, 55-56, 110, 129, 143, 150, 151, 154; relations with Soviet mission, 118-19, 131-32, 137-38, 168; relations with Germans, 130, 133-42, 145; arrest, 131-38

H

Hanecki, Jakob, 86
Herzog, Jakob (1892-1931), 3, 34, 142-43, 155
Hoffmann, Hermann Arthur (1857-1927), 24, 26, 130
Holzmann, Eduard (1882-

1936), Soviet courier, 16, 41, 46-52, 55, 57, 59, 76, 78, 81, 101, 104, 113-14, 125, 130, 131, 132
Humbert-Droz, Jules (1891-1972), 3, 37-38, 83, 137, 144, 182

I

Inglesia, Pablo, 122
International Socialist Commission, 3, 14-15, 21, 35, 86, 99, 121, 122, 148, 150, 151
Itschner, Hans, 34

J

Jacob, Jeanne (1885-   ), 126-27, 133
Joffe, Adolf A. (1883-1927), Soviet representative in Berlin, 3-4, 5, 13, 20, 52, 59, 61, 62-63, 74-78, 87, 88, 107, 149, 153, 161, 176
Jordi, Hans (1885-   ), 117
Jungburschen, 31-34, 38, 164
Junod, Albert, 90-92, 177-78

K

Kaclerovič, Triša, 126
Kahan, Adam (1881-   ), 109
Kamenev, L. B. (1883-1936), 52-54, 59, 60
Kamkov, Boris, 108
Karklin, P. E. (1882-1919), 175

218 *Index*

Karpinsky, V. A. (1880-   ),
16, 18, 42, 49
Kautsky, Karl (1854-1938),
113
Kollontaj, A. M. (1872-1952),
21
Krupskaya, N. K. (1869-1939),
60, 102, 116

L

Lamm, R. A., 102
Lang, Otto (1863-1936), 162-
64
Leeper, Rex, 44
Left Socialist Revolutionaries,
105-8, 172
Legien, Carl, 139
Leiteisen, M. G. (1897-1939),
Berzin's secretary, 64, 131-
32, 135
Lenin, Vladimir Ilich (1870-
1924), Bolshevik leader, 1,
6-11, 12, 17-20, 21, 102,
109-10, 117-18, 119, 129,
131-32, 135, 151; and mission in Stockholm, 15; and
Swiss socialists, 30, 31, 33,
37, 86-87, 142-43; assassination attempts, 31, 106, 139;
and Berzin, 60, 77, 96,
111-13, 159
Lifschitz, Boris (1879-   ),
71, 97
Lipnitsky, Baruch, 56-57, 122,
132-33, 134
Litvinov, M. M. (1876-1951),
16, 42-45, 46, 53-54, 63,
65, 92
Liubarskaia, 177-78

Liubarsky, Nikolai, secretary
of Soviet mission, 64, 98,
99, 114, 122, 123-24, 138,
150, 155, 182
Lockhart, Robert Bruce, British agent in Russia, 44, 81,
91-92, 100-101
London, Soviet mission in, 1,
3, 16
Lunacharsky, A. V. (1875-
1933), 116, 129

M

MacDonald, Ramsay, 121
Maklakov, V. A., 29
Mercier, Philipp, Swiss minister
in Berlin, 61-63, 74-77, 149
Miliukov, P. N. (1859-1943),
29
Miliutin, V. (1884-1938), 90,
171
Milkich, Ilia (1884-   ),
Serbian socialist, 126-27,
133, 182
Mirbach, Wilhelm (1871-1918),
German ambassador to
Soviet Russia, 85, 88, 106
Misiano, Francesco, Italian
socialist, 35-36, 38, 56, 123-
24, 152
Moor, Karl Vital (1852-1932),
Swiss socialist, 61, 85-90,
95
Moscow, Swiss consulate in,
59, 74
Motta, Giuseppe (1871-1940),
25, 162
Müller, Eduard (1848-1919),

25, 67, 68, 138, 158, 159,
162-64
Münzenberg, Willi (1889-
1940), 3, 31-35, 38, 52, 88,
129, 179

N

Nabokov, Constantine, 43
Naine, Charles, 103
Natanson, Mark A. (1850-
1919), Left Socialist Revolutionary, 21, 60, 75-77,
105-8, 150, 153-54, 172
Neue Zürcher Zeitung, 26, 38,
109, 116, 140
Nobs, Ernst (1886-1957), 31,
35, 95, 126-27, 141, 145
Nogueira, Cesar, 121
Nouvelle Internationale, La,
37, 57, 118, 130, 134, 138,
142
Noverraz, Gustave, 135

O

Odier, Edouard, Swiss minister
in Russia, 41, 42, 54, 88,
92-94, 99, 177, 178
Onu, A. M., Russian consul in
London, 43
Onu, Andrei Mikhailovich,
Russian diplomat in Bern,
28-29, 41, 66-73, 80, 81,
104

P

Pageot (Colonel), French military attaché, 26-27, 39, 56,

89, 91, 98, 129-30, 131,
132, 134-35, 138, 139, 143-
44, 147, 150-51, 155, 156,
159-60, 169
Paravicini, Charles R., director
of Swiss Foreign Office, 66-
69, 73, 77, 90, 95, 136-37,
157, 158, 163-64
Parvus, A. L. (Helfand), 130
Peluso, Edmondo (1882-1942),
112, 116, 120-22
Peters, William, 101
Peterson, Albert, 64
Petrograd, Entente diplomats
in, 10, 12, 16-17, 24, 41,
42-43
Petropavlovsky, Sergei, 98,
114-15
Petrov, Peter, 17-18
Pichon, Stephen, 156
Platten, Fritz (1883-1942),
Swiss socialist, 3, 31, 49-50,
51, 55, 56, 83, 94, 95, 99,
114, 119, 122, 125, 127,
142, 153, 155, 162-64, 168,
170, 171, 180, 182
Pokrovskaia, Liubov, 64, 96,
98, 99, 114, 115, 122
Popov, Semion, 64
Price, Morgan Philips, 118
Promachos Verlag, 117-18

R

Radek, Karl (1885-1941), 86,
107, 118, 180
recognition of Soviet regime,
by Swiss, 1, 5, 41, 64-70,
87, 94; by English, 41-45,
67

Red Cross, 84, 102-5, 123, 125, 148, 158, 162, 163-64
Reich, James (1886-   ), 114-17, 119, 120, 122, 124, 125, 155, 177, 182
Rembelinsky, Vladimir, 103
Revoluzzer, Der, 34
Rivlina, Elizabeth, 64
Rivosh, Maximilian, 82, 83, 98, 99
Robins, Raymond, 18
Rolland, Romain (1866-1944), 37, 83, 118-19, 137
Romberg, Gisbert von (1866-1939), 27, 83, 86-88
Rosenberg, Jacques Gabriel von, 133-34, 136, 140
ROSTA, 125
Rumbold, Horace, 25, 64, 68, 72-73, 93-94, 109, 147, 176
Russian Information Bureau, Bern, 126-27
Russische Nachrichten, 113-25, 171, 177

S

Sacerdote, Gustavo, 36, 48, 50, 56, 152
Sadoul, Jacques, 118-19
Scheidemann, Philipp, 139
Schlesinger, Paul, 133-35, 136, 138, 140, 151, 154
Schneider, Friedrich, 145
Schulthess, Edmund (1868-1944), 25, 68, 88-89, 91, 162
Schweide, Isaak, 122-24, 155, 177, 179

Sentinelle, La, 37-38, 108, 137, 141, 142, 144
Shaikovich, Abraham, 48
Shklovskaia, Dvasia (1880-   ), 66, 177, 178
Shklovsky, G. L. (1875-1937), 64-68, 70, 73, 77, 86, 95, 96-98, 109-10, 124, 136, 150, 157, 170, 171, 172, 176
Shneerson, Ilia, 103
Shreider, Alexander (1891-   ), 105-8, 144, 172
slogans: "immediate peace without annexations and without indemnities," 6-7, 8-9, 20; abolition of secret diplomacy, 8, 44; revolutionary war, 9, 17, 20, 184; "breathing space," 17; "no war, no peace," 19; support of the October Revolution, 20
Snowden, Philip, 121
Sokolnikov, G. Ia., 37
soldiers, Russian, in Switzerland, 47, 49, 70, 84, 101-5, 150, 152, 154, 162, 163
Soloviev, Iu. Ia., 83
Sonnino, Sidney, 156
Spitteler, Carl (1845-1924), 23
Starke, Peters, 64, 98
Steinberg, Isaac, 105-8, 172
Stepankovsky, Vladimir (1885-1941), 120-21
Stockholm, Soviet mission in, 1, 2, 4, 14-15, 22, 48
Stockholm, Swiss consulate in, 148-49

Stovall, Pleasant A., 25, 28, 79-80, 181
students, Russian, in Switzerland, 80, 82
Studer, Fritz, 142, 171
Suter, Friedrich, 74, 102, 106
Svatikov, S. G., 28
Sverdlov, Ia. M. (1885-1919), 112
Sviatkovsky, Vsevolod, 81
Swiss Socialist Party, 30, 38-39, 86, 126, 140, 141-42, 143, 157, 162-63, 167, 180
Switzerland: neutrality, 23, 26, 40, 135, 161; nationality problems, 23, 24; investments in Russia, 42, 147; relations with Soviet government, 2, 41-42, 84-85, 89-90, 92-94, 168-69, 179-80; Bolshevik views of, 21-22

T

Thurnheer, Walter, 65, 95, 173
Troelstra, Pieter, 139
Trotsky, L. D. (1879-1940), 8-10, 12, 17, 18-19, 41, 44, 46, 117, 118, 119, 126, 129

U

Übersax, Fritz, 126

V

Viktorov-Toporov, V., 29
Visani, Domenico, 36, 152
Vogel, Hans, 142
Volksrecht, 108, 141

Vorovsky, V. V. (1871-1923), 4, 14-15, 22, 45, 46, 48, 50, 54, 59, 65, 87, 114, 179

W

Waibel, Toni, 34, 136
Walecki, Maximilian G. (Horwitz), 50
Welti, Franz, 171
Wetzosol, Julius (Vecozols, 1884-1945), 114, 125, 177
Wille, Ulrich (1848-1925), 23, 166-67, 170
Wilson, Woodrow, 17, 179

Z

Zalkind, Ivan A. (1885-1928), 5, 60, 81; Deputy Commissar of Foreign Affairs, 11-12, 18; travels to Switzerland, 46, 52-57, 59, 61-62; activity in Switzerland, 73, 98-99, 105, 109-10, 114, 118, 131-33, 134-35, 138-39, 150; troubles with Swiss authorities and expulsion, 136, 157, 158, 159, 162, 171, 174
Zamiatin, Nikolai, 113-14, 116
Zimmerwald movement, 3, 14, 21, 30, 57, 60, 86, 120, 130, 133, 139, 140, 148, 151; Zimmerwald Left, 30, 31, 39, 60
Zurich, radicals in, 30-36, 38, 50, 136, 142-43, 168-69